The
WORD
for the
WEEK

D1713815

53 Weekly Meditations
with Daily Scripture Moments

Dr. Todd Stiles

To the faithful flock at First Family Church who have heard this refrain more than any of us can count — "It's the Word that does the work"— thank you for craving, hearing, digesting, obeying and sharing the life-changing truth of Scripture with me all these years and being a body that truly believes 1 Thessalonians 2:13.

Contents

How To Utilize this Simple Book

This book is a supplement.

It's not meant to replace your current and regular reading of the Bible, nor is it meant to be a substitute for your deeper study of the Scriptures.

It is simply meant to act as an additive, giving you an extra opportunity to meditate on the Word in a meaningful, succinct fashion six days of the week.

Here's how it works: Each Monday, take 5 minutes and read the meditation, as well as the Scripture referenced in it. Then, Tuesday through Saturday, take 2 minutes and read the verse or verses listed by that day after the meditation. Perhaps it's over coffee before you start your day; maybe during lunch. Maybe before bed, during dinner, or during an afternoon break at work or while your children are napping. Regardless, schedule a few moments for a bite of the Bible.

Why? Because it's the Word that does the work. Ingest it. Digest it. As you do, your character will be refined and your life defined.

That's the way to get the most out of this simple book over the next 365 days. By God's grace, you will.

Todd

WEEK 1
Which Traits Matter?

Many things are important. Few things are essential.

For instance, air conditioning is important. Air is essential.

Hot water is important. Water is essential.

Driving home this very point relationally was a 2020 study done among Iowa church members. They were surveyed about five servant leadership traits exhibited in their pastors—love, humility, trust, vision, and empowerment—to see if any of these traits were correlated to the intention of the members to stay connected and involved in the church.

The result? All were correlated to congregational retention. What was surprising, however, was that two of the traits were beyond the level of correlation. The research indicated two traits were at the level of predictability, the highest level possible in quantitative research. Those 2 traits? Love (with a predictability score of .000) and humility (with a predictability score of .009).

The point? Pastors who exhibit love and humility see a higher rate of retention among their members. I'd venture to say that also equates, eventually, to deeper relationships, wider impact, and stronger ministry. Truly, many traits matter. But two, apparently, matter most.

Not surprising is this: our Lord has already told us this. Meditate on these words for a moment:

> "Now the goal of our instruction is love that comes from a pure heart." (1 Timothy 1:5)
> "Do nothing out of selfish ambition or conceit, but in humility consider others as more important than yourselves." (Phil. 2:3)

"Now these three remain: faith, hope, and love— but the greatest of these is love." (1 Cor. 13:13)

As I poured over those findings, remembering that Jesus had told us these things already, I couldn't help but ponder the difference love and humility could make in other relational environments, such as our families and friendships. I'd venture to say the findings from this research are generally transferable, and that people in general respond quite favorably to expressions of love and humility from those with whom they interact. No doubt many traits could be important. Two will be essential.

This year, pursue important qualities, but especially love and humility. Give and live sacrificially. Put others first. Meet needs. Defer credit. Accept responsibility instead of blaming. Build others up, don't tear them down. Express sincere gratefulness, not proud criticism. These are just a few of the practical ways you can serve others through love and humility, tightening the bond of your relationships in the coming year.

Tuesday
John 13:12-14

Wednesday
1 Peter 4:10

Thursday
Galatians 5:13-14

Friday
Hebrews 10:24

Saturday/Sunday
Philippians 2:3-4

"No doubt many traits could be important. Two will be essential: Love and humility."

WEEK 2
Greatly Loved

God does what he does because of who he is. His character always informs his actions.

Not only does this mean God operates fully and eternally in perfect and righteous ways, but it further means God isn't leveraged or manipulated by outside forces. This does not mean God isn't moved or touched by our condition. Rather, that because our condition and situation is known by God, and because he is who he is, he responds to us on the basis of his own essence, not on the basis of our exertion.

This is clearly seen in many Scriptures, where we are told God moves and acts on our behalf out of his own character, not because of our conduct. Notice just a few of the more obvious ones and let them warm your heart for a moment:

> "But God, being rich in mercy, because of the great love with which he loved us, even when we were dead in our trespasses, made us alive together with Christ—by grace you have been saved." (Ephesians 2:4-5)
> "For God so loved the world, that he gave his only Son, that whoever believes in him should not perish but have eternal life." (John 3:16)
> "But God shows his love for us in that while we were still sinners, Christ died for us." (Romans 5:8)

A more obscure reference to this same theological truth is found in Daniel. In fact, three times we see the phrase "you are greatly loved" (9:23, 10:11, 10:23), indicating that each time God gifted Daniel with divine insight into visions and mysteries, it wasn't due to anything Daniel did. Instead, it was solely because of God's great affection for Daniel.

How reassuring and comforting to know that God bestows his blessings on us because he has made us his beloved. That's right—the action is all God's from start to finish. Whatever gifts and good we receive, it is due to the lavish grace of God.

Rejoice today, my fellow recipient of God's undeserved yet displayed kindness, that "every good and perfect gift comes from the Father above" (James 1:17), and live in light of the unconditional love and favor of our Lord. Yes, you, too, are greatly loved!

Tuesday
Romans 8:38-39

Wednesday
Ephesians 3:18-19

Thursday
Psalm 36:5-7

Friday
2 Corinthians 5:14-15

Saturday/Sunday
Psalm 31:7

"God responds to us on the basis of his own essence, not on the basis of our exertion."

WEEK 3
Finally Fully Blameless

Being "blameless" is not only biblical. It's beautiful.

Consider these exhortations: Believers are exhorted to live blamelessly as lights in the world (Phil. 2:15), the Hebrew hymnbook declares a blessing upon blameless people (Psalm 119:1), and men who desire to shepherd the church (i.e., elders) and serve the church (i.e., deacons) are required to be blameless (1 Tim 3:2, 10).

Yet, I bet you'd admit with me that blamelessness seems practically impossible. Who hasn't caused injury or brought pain to someone who would point at us accusingly and hold us liable? No doubt all of us know someone who could pin us down with the verdict, "This was your fault." Sure, forgiveness reconciles, and restoration is a beautifully necessary pursuit in these kinds of times. Still, the reality that various kinds and degrees of trauma have occurred, and could still occur, due to the ongoing battle that is warring between our old and new natures, can leave us burdened under the weight of a goal that seems elusive and unattainable.

That very thought is why I delight so deeply in 1 Thessalonians 3:13, which assures us there is a day coming when our hearts will be established "blameless in holiness." Take a moment and let the entire context of verses 12-13 wash over you:

> "...may the Lord make you increase and abound in love for one another and for all, as we do for you, so that he may establish your hearts blameless in holiness before our God and Father, at the coming of our Lord Jesus with all his saints."

While Paul exhorts them to love one another more and more in the present, he is fully aware that the pinnacle moment when they will experience full and lasting blamelessness—permanent blamelessness—is in the future, specifically when Jesus returns. He points them towards Christ's coming as a means of motivation, encouraging them to persevere and endure in their pursuit of blamelessness, knowing that our up-and down efforts now are not the final word on the matter. That final word belongs to God who will, at the coming of Jesus, once and for all settle the matter for everyone who belongs to him. That word? Blameless. Fully. Finally. And forever.

So love strongly today. Seek unity fervently. Make amends quickly. Forgive readily. Yes, live as blameless as you can in a fallen world as a redeemed, yet fallen human being. But do so, not as a means of achieving God's ultimate affirmation, but rather in anticipation of what he knows you already are positionally and will, at Jesus' return, lavish upon you personally and practically: blameless.

Tuesday
Jude 24-25

Wednesday
1 Corinthians 1:8

Thursday
Ephesians 5:27

Friday
Colossians 1:22

Saturday/Sunday
1 Thessalonians 5:23

"Our up-and down efforts now are not the final word on the matter of blamelessness. That final word belongs to God who will, at the coming of Jesus, once and for all settle the matter for everyone who belongs to him."

WEEK 4
There are no Little Sins

Refuse to believe the lie that sins are measured by size.

The truth is this: there are no little sins.

Paul takes direct aim at this concept when, after warning the Ephesian believers about the clear and present danger of sexual sin (Ephesians 4:19), he also exhorts them to resist the less apparent sins of lying, bitterness, and shouting, commanding they be "removed from you" (4:25-31).

He follows this same pattern in chapter 5, reminding the church that not one hint of sexual immorality should be named among them. But neither should there be any seed of greed. Wage war against both.

Essentially, Paul clearly and collectively groups both outward sin, what we often falsely refer to as "big," with inward sin, what we unfortunately label as "little." Both are deceitfully dangerous and destructively deadly and should be resisted equally. When we see sin in terms of size, assuming there are "little lies" or "quick looks" that don't matter, we fall into the very trap Satan has set.

I suspect this may be how Adam and Eve fell for the forbidden fruit (Genesis 3). Convinced deceitfully by Satan that God wouldn't carry out his promised punishment if they disobeyed (3:4), perhaps they reasoned to themselves, "It's just one bite. Death seems harsh for such a small infraction." But that one sinful bite plunged them, and every person born thereafter, into death and depravity.

Seeing sin in sizes may be why Achan took some of the spoils from Jericho, even though the Lord clearly commanded every

Israelite not to take any of the battle's leftovers (Joshua 6:18-19). Perhaps he assumed it was just one simple nugget of gold. Just one nice garment. Just one handful of silver. But the next day, he and his entire family paid a large price for what he thought, at the time, was a small sin—death.

It's no surprise, then, that James would write the following words about all sin: when it is finished, it brings forth death (James 1:14). Every sin is a noose from your enemy, the Devil. And there are no lifesaving nooses. Every one of them kills.

Today and this week, resist the temptation to categorize your sin as "big" and "little." Refuse to think some matter, others don't. See all sin as deadly, and commit to, by the power of God's Spirit and God's Word, killing it, not managing it.

Tuesday
Ephesians 4:31-32

Wednesday
1 Peter 5:8

Thursday
1 John 1:7-9

Friday
1 Corinthians 10:13

Saturday/Sunday
Probers 28:13

"When we see sin in terms of size, assuming there are 'little lies' or 'quick looks' that don't matter, we fall into the very trap Satan has set."

WEEK 5
Gospel Encouragement

When grief strikes, the gospel sustains. When sorrow engulfs, the gospel encourages.

This is the principle underneath the call to "encourage one another with these words." This phrase, the last in a section of verses that closes out 1 Thessalonians 4, rests upon a number of promises about those who have died in Christ, promises that provide deep and abiding comfort in the midst of grief and sorrow. This is what "these words" refer to, and it reads as follows:

> For we say this to you by a word from the Lord: We who are still alive at the Lord's coming will certainly not precede those who have fallen asleep. For the Lord himself will descend from heaven with a shout, with the archangel's voice, and with the trumpet of God, and the dead in Christ will rise first. Then we who are still alive, who are left, will be caught up together with them in the clouds to meet the Lord in the air, and so we will always be with the Lord. (1 Thess. 4:15-17)

But on what basis does God make these promises that comfort and encourage his people in times of bereavement? What is the foundation for "these words" which guarantee a hopeful future? The basis is found in verse 14, one of the first phrases in the section — "For if we believe that Jesus died and rose again." The guarantee that death is not the end for all who believe is the truth that Jesus is no longer dead. His resurrection assures us of ours; his victory over the grave promises us we will experience one, too. We are comforted in death because he has conquered death.

This is why we can positively and unquestionably state that when grief strikes, the gospel sustains. When grief engulfs, the gospel encourages. Truly, it's the death and resurrection of Jesus that is the core element of sustaining comfort.

If you wondered, when your believing loved one passed in death, if you'd ever see them again, or questioned if you'd be reunited with your fellow follower of Jesus who suddenly died, the answer is a most definitive yes! The historical and supernatural death and resurrection of Jesus Christ in real time and space—the gospel—means those who have trusted in him but have gone through death's door will experience the same thing when he returns—a resurrection in real time and space.

How beautifully and powerfully God's good news turns our sorrow to hope. How deeply grateful we are that when grief strikes, the gospel sustains; that when grief engulfs, the gospel encourages.

Tuesday
1 Corinthians 15:1-4, 20-22

Wednesday
Philippians 3:20-21

Thursday
John 14:1-3

Friday
Romans 8:38-39

Saturday / Sunday
John 11:25-26

"We are comforted in death because he has conquered death."

WEEK 6
Sending is Trinitarian

Sending isn't just a missionary task. It is a trinitarian concept.

Consider this: The Father sent the Son (John 20:21), and the Father and the Son sent the Spirit (John 14:26 and 15:26). So when the Son and Spirit sent the church (John 20:21; Acts 1:8), it was not a new phenomenon. It was an eternal aspect of the Godhead further on display. Sending is grounded in the Trinity.

In fact, did you know Jesus is referred to as the sent one 40 times in the book of John? And that in the narrative of Cornelius (Acts 10), Luke uses send 11 times? Add to this that the final words of Jesus to his disciples, which drip with the clear command to carry on the mission for which he was sent, is described in every single one of the gospels, as well as the book of Acts? Sending isn't an "add-on" to the Christian faith. It's at the heart of the Godhead and a core theme of the Scriptures.

This undoubtedly escalates sending among the Christian's, and church's, priorities. It isn't optional, but rather essential. And while there may be a variety of ways to send or be sent, disregarding both isn't an alternative. It's disobedience, an action that misrepresents the very nature of God.

It isn't surprising, then, that Jesus would assume the act of going, or being sent, when he commanded his followers to "make disciples of all nations" (Matthew 28:18-20). "Go" isn't really the decision at hand; it's already concluded. It is presumed and considered underway. We are a sent people by nature of the God who redeemed us. The question is, as we are going (i.e., sent), will we make disciples of all nations?

This week, as you encounter all kinds of people, live as a sent one representing the Trinitarian God. Conduct yourself as an ambassador on-mission from your true country, God's kingdom. Live and give as one empowered by the Holy Spirit to see Christ's name preached in places it has yet to be heard.

In the plainest of words, share your story of salvation. Testify to God's grace. Give sacrificially. Intentionally go places to develop relationships with those who are far from God so that they may be drawn to God. Schedule your day and week with God's mission in mind. In both word and action, let's reflect the sending work of the Godhead so that all may know the saving work of the Godhead.

Tuesday
John 20:21

Wednesday
Isaiah 6:8

Thursday
Matthew 4:19

Friday
Romans 10:15

Saturday/Sunday
John 17:18

"Sending isn't an 'add-on' to the Christian faith. It's at the heart of the Godhead and a core theme of the Scriptures."

WEEK 7
It's not an Interruption

Suffering is often the intended way of proclaiming the gospel, not simply a secondary result of proclaiming it.

Paul makes this precise point in Philippians 1:12 when he writes, "Now I want you to know, brothers and sisters, that what has happened to me has actually advanced the gospel."

The key word is "actually," indicating Paul was helping his readers think correctly about his imprisonment. For Paul, his suffering and imprisonment weren't interruptions, a mere consequence of preaching the gospel; it was the conduit for preaching the gospel. To whom? As 1:13 says, the "whole imperial guard." Apparently, God knew it would take prison time for Paul to get preaching time with certain soldiers and officials. It would take chains on Paul for some to hear of Christ through Paul.

This is deeply comforting and boldly reassuring. God's sovereign hand in all things means that what I view as a consequence—difficulty and suffering—God is actually using as a conduit. What I often see as an effect from others, God may actually be using to affect others. What I think is an interruption is actually divinely intentional. God is purposeful in everything that he allows into my life, not accidental. And one of those purposes—intents—is that others may hear and know of him.

As you consider your hard situations today, live with the confidence that your less-than-desirable encounters and hard-to-process experiences are not random interruptions. They are not chance coincidences. Instead, they are the sovereign avenues—intentional conduits and divine doorways—by which God is providentially and powerfully accomplishing his purposes in you and through you for the spread of his glory and the fame of his name.

Tuesday
Genesis 50:20

Wednesday
1 Peter 5:10

Thursday
James 1:12

Friday
2 Corinthians 4:17

Saturday/Sunday
Isaiah 43:2

"God is purposeful in everything that he allows into my life, not accidental. And one of those purposes—intents—is that others may hear and know of him."

WEEK 8
Everybody Needs a Jim

Two can carry a burden better than one.

Such is the thought behind Galatians 6:2, where the Apostle Paul exhorted believers to "bear one another's burdens." There's something beautiful about an extra shoulder that shows up when the load is beyond our capacity.

For Bob, that shoulder belonged to a man named Jim.

Bob was a young pastor experiencing the various ups and downs of a small, rural church. One day, while praying for the flock during an intense time of church strife, he sensed a strong prompting from the Holy Spirit to go by and see Jim, an older gentleman in the church. Assuming it was for Jim's sake, Bob dropped in on Jim, only to be met with an outstretched hand that offered a Coke and an invitation to stay for a bit.

"I was expecting you," Jim said, asking next, "Wanna talk?"

Bob did precisely that.

What followed was unconditional love and a listening ear from Jim. He was present for and with Bob. Jim was the load-bearing friend that God brought around at just the right time, the hands that helped carry the burdens that would have otherwise buried Bob.

For over a year, Bob would "drop in" on Jim, and every time Bob was greeted with the outstretched hand that held a Coke and the burden-bearing shoulder that held some of the weight. As Bob would tearfully describe it later, "Jim was an oasis from God in my pastoral desert. He was a refreshing friend who bore the burden with me."

Is there a 'Bob' in your life? What could you do today to help bear the burdens of that person? In what ways could you flesh out Galatians 6:1 in that relationship? Consider an encouraging call or text. A delicious meal. A simple gift. An edifying conversation. Even a Coke.

After all, everybody needs a Jim.

Tuesday
Galatians 6:2

Wednesday
Proverbs 18:24

Thursday
1 Thessalonians 5:11

Friday
Proverbs 12:25

Saturday/Sunday
Romans 15:1-2

"There's something beautiful about an extra shoulder that shows up when the load is beyond our capacity."

WEEK 9
Diotrephes or Demetrius?

Are you a selfish divider or a selfless edifier?

This was the juxtaposition John drew in his third letter as he contrasted Diotrephes—the selfish divider—with Demetrius—the selfless edifier.

Known as one who "likes to put himself first" (3 John 1:9-11), Diotrephes refused to acknowledge church authority, and spoke wickedly and nonsensical about Christ's body. Instead of welcoming others, he refused them, especially the traveling missionaries, and even expelled those in the church who were wanting to be hospitable to them. No wonder John said he would, when he came, "bring up what he is doing," meaning John was planning on exposing Diotrephes' wrong motives and behavior.

Demetrius, on the other hand, was one who visibly supported the authority and actions of the church. He had received "a good testimony from everyone" (3 John 1:12), indicating all the church knew Demetrius was selflessly synced up with the church's work and leaders. John even said "the truth itself" lined up with how Demetrius behaved, meaning his life was humbly in line with God's Word and united with God's mission. To top it off, John adds his own approval, letting the readers know Demetrius was the kind of man he could trust. Consequently, so could they.

No doubt John provided a contrast of character for us. He also provided a contrast of reaction: One was corrected; the other commended.

Interestingly, both were in the church. As much as we'd all like to think the church in this current generation, both universally and locally, is an exception, the stark reality is that we're not. Both kinds of people exist in our churches still today. Which is why I asked you earlier: Are you a selfish divider or a selfless edifier? Are you a Diotrephes or a Demetrius? Are you headed for correction or commendation?

If you find yourself more like the first, ask God to forgive you for your divisive rebellion and start afresh today edifying and unifying the body of Christ. In fact, reach out to a fellow member who needs encouragement today and do exactly that—encourage them now!

If you find yourself more like the second, keep obeying the call to selfless edification in an increasing fashion. Continue ordering your life in such a way that the rest of God's people know you live in line with God's Word and God's mission.

Oh, for an endless number of men and women living like Demetrius, not Diotrephes.

Tuesday
Psalm 133:1

Wednesday
Romans 14:19

Thursday
2 Corinthians 13:11

Friday
Acts 4:32

Saturday/Sunday
1 Peter 3:8

"Are you a selfish divider or a selfless edifier? Are you headed for correction or commendation?"

WEEK 10
Trusting Even When Tested

Why Peter and not James?

That was the question that raced to the forefront of my mind when I finished reading the first 11 verses of Acts 12. In that passage, two opposite things occurred: James was arrested and executed by Herod, but Peter was arrested and freed by an angel.

See what I mean? I bet you're wondering the same thing—*Why Peter and not James?*

Let's be quick to admit we don't know. Scripture doesn't give us the answer. What the Bible does show us implicitly is that those early believers in Jerusalem were not deterred from trusting even when they were tested. How do we know? They gathered to pray at Mary's house when they got the news of Peter's arrest. In the middle of unexpected crises and unanswered questions, the church of the first century stayed on their knees to God instead of turning their backs on God.

More than likely, you have an "Acts 12" scenario in your life.

- Why did I get cancer, but not him?
- Why did she keep her job, but not me?
- Why is my child terminally ill, but not theirs?
- Why are my parents suffering in the older years, but not his?
- Why did my pregnancy end in a miscarriage, but not my friends?

Life's journey is dotted with moments when we have questions with no answers; when we realize we're going through a trial. In that moment of testing, will your response indicate your continued trust in God? This is exactly what prayer does—reveals our continued dependence upon the Lord.

No wonder prayer is our first and best action. Nothing showcases our continued trust in Christ, even when we're tested, like a bent knee and a cry for help.

Today, if things go like you hope, pray. If they don't, pray. If you have a James-like tragedy, pray. If you have a Peter-like victory, pray. Whatever occurs, pray without ceasing to ensure you trust while tested.

Tuesday
Psalm 143:8

Wednesday
James 1:12

Thursday
Psalm 9:10

Friday
Romans 8:28

Saturday/Sunday
Proverbs 3:5-6

"Nothing showcases our continued trust in Christ, even when we're tested, like a bent knee and a cry for help."

WEEK 11
Buying Back Opportunities

Hanging on a wall in my office is a replica of the world's first concept of a calendar. It was developed by the Egyptians, and shows the intersections of the annual seasons, the 12 months, and even the different weeks within those months. It's quite fascinating!

It's also quite convicting.

Every time I glance at that reproduction of an ancient time piece, I'm reminded, sometimes even reprimanded, to invest into eternity, not simply consume in the moment. How easy it is to spend time, even waste it.

We are called to something higher and greater when it comes to time—to "make the best use of it" (Ephesians 5:16). One translation refers to it as "redeeming the time," another as "making the most of your time." In each rendering, the overwhelming sense of the text is that time is an asset, not a liability. It can produce a return if used wisely.

This is precisely why, in the same set of verses, Paul exhorts believers to "walk as wise" people who "understand what the the will of the Lord is" (5:15, 17). The best investment of our time occurs when we pour it into God's purposes, the things that are on his agenda and heart. Truly, when our calendars and clocks are aligned with God's character and callings, we're not just spending time; we're buying back time and putting it to its greatest possible use.

As you travel through the rest of this day, think beyond a mere chronological sequence of numbers. Know that what lies before you is a biblical opportunity to gain the greatest eternal return through the wise investment of temporal blocks of time. When we leverage all of our moments, hours, days and weeks to that end, we will be doing more than managing our time. We will be making the most of it.

Tuesday
Psalm 90:12

Wednesday
Colossians 4:5

Thursday
2 Corinthians 4:18

Friday
Ecclesiastes 3:11

Saturday/Sunday
Proverbs 27:1

"The best investment of our time occurs when we pour it into God's purposes."

WEEK 12
God's Unconditional Love

God's love is qualitatively and quantitatively different than our love. Need proof? Consider the first part of 1 John 3:1.

> "See what kind of love the Father has given to us, that we should be called children of God; and so we are."

When John wrote "what kind of love," he was literally referring to it as "other worldly love," indicating it's not something we've humanly known or seen. And for good reason—because of God's love, we have been brought into the family of God. What an incredible and miraculous reality that spiritual enemies of God can actually become spiritual "children of God." No wonder his response to this kind of love was "See!" One translation begins this verse with the word, "Behold." In our common vernacular, we'd probably say, "Stop and take a look at this!" No matter how you slice it, John is calling for a long look at the love of God.

Why? Because no other love goes to such dramatically great lengths for those are the epitome of unlovely. Think about it— God moved towards us when we we're fighting against him. God reached out to us when we were rejecting him. God wanted the best for us when we were at our worst. God did everything necessary to save those who were doing everything to sin. That's the kind of love he has for us: unconditional.

It's this unconditional love that is at the root of God's redemptive actions. John says this is why he sent his only Son (John 3:16), and Paul asserted this is why Christ died for us (Romans 5:8) and why God made us alive with Christ (Ephesians 2:5). These cornerstone actions of salvation were not aimed at people who were deserving or worthy, individuals who had earned some type of divine extra credit. They were on behalf of the weak, the ungodly, and the sinful (Romans 5:6-8). There were no conditions that needed met before God would love us. He loved us out of his own compassion, what the Bible calls his "rich mercy" and "great love" (Ephesians 2:4).

When we look long at this kind of love from God, we will begin to be motivated by it. It will begin to "control us" (2 Cor. 5:14), enabling us to love more and more like God—unconditionally. To love, not just in word, but "in deed and in truth" (1 John 3:18). We will notice a proactive spirit welling up within us to take loving action in spite of who people are, not just because of who people are.

This week, savor the unconditional love of God that was showcased in the person of Jesus, God's only Son. Let it sink deeply down into your soul, recalibrating how you love and live while you wait with eagerness for his second coming.

Tuesday
Jude 21

Wednesday
Psalm 36:7

Thursday
1 Corinthians 13:13

Friday
1 John 4:9-10

Saturday/Sunday
John 15:13

"There were no conditions that needed met before God would love us."

WEEK 13
Salvation Belongs to the Lord

Salvation is solely and wholly a work of God.

That 9-word, labor-freeing, heart-melting, praise-producing, soul-satisfying refrain occupied my attention in a heightened manner during 2010 as I preached through Romans and documented the salvation stories of several of our church members. It eventually turned into the somewhat free-verse poem *"Salvation Belongs to the Lord,"* which I wrote and titled after Psalm 3:8.

The poem's repetition also served as a sort of meditation for me, allowing me to verbally "chew" on the same phrase and concept over and over. (Transparently, my heart has set it to music at times, but never to the same tune; that's a sign it should probably remain a meditative poem, right?)

Still, no matter if I sang it or said it, I found increased gratitude, deepened praise, and intensified commitment. It's my prayer this theological tribute to God's complete ownership of salvation will do the same for you this week.

"Salvation Belongs to the Lord"

It's not because how hard I try,
but only because you choose to die
and free me from my sin.
Through you I'm born again.

It's not because of what I've earned,
but only because you choose to turn
and breathe your life in me.
Through you I'm finally free.

Only through you, Jesus! Only to you Jesus!
Salvation belongs to the Lord!
Only through you, Jesus! Only to you Jesus!
Salvation belongs to the Lord!

It's not because of who I am,
but only because the Great I AM
rescued me from death
and set my sights on heav'n.

Condemned forever by the fall,
Yet Jesus' blood has paid it all
and ransomed me from hell.
In Christ my soul is well!

Only through you, Jesus! Only to you Jesus!
Salvation belongs to the Lord!
Only through you, Jesus! Only to you Jesus!
Salvation belongs to the Lord!

We raise our hallelujahs, we lift our praises to you!
We only boast in the power of your name.
We raise our hallelujahs, we lift our praises to you!
We solely cling to Calvary unashamed.

Only through you, Jesus! Only to you Jesus!
Salvation belongs to the Lord!
Only through you, Jesus! Only to you Jesus!
Salvation belongs to the Lord!

Tuesday
Romans 1:16

Wednesday
1 Thessalonians 5:9-10

Thursday
John 1:12-13

Friday
Psalm 79:9

Saturday/Sunday
Ephesians 2:8-9

"Salvation is solely and wholly a work of God."

WEEK 14
Why Jesus Makes Himself Known

Jesus makes himself known so that you will faithfully believe and fearlessly follow.

I draw this from John 21, where twice we read in the first 14 verses that Jesus "revealed" (21:1, 14) himself to the disciples. The word *revealed* serves as a bookend of sorts to help us understand the intent of Jesus—to clearly disclose his post-resurrection reality and make known to them his power and authority.

As a disciple, Peter experienced this personally, taking steps of obedience and action in response to the revealing of Jesus. He was the first to get to the shore to see Jesus (21:4-8), and he was the first to get the fish to the fire for cooking (21:9-11). Peter was seeing Jesus' authority and power on display. His response was beautifully spontaneous: "I'm in!"

It's quite clear that Jesus wasn't going to let Peter wallow in the failure and rejection of that previous night of denial; he would not allow him to live in the shadow of his regretted past. Jesus was intentionally calling him back to a life of faith, taking the first step in this restoration by showing Peter unmistakably that he had a future and a hope for him (21:15-19). And both were in following Jesus obediently and fearlessly.

This is the way Jesus works. He continually makes himself known to us through his Word and by his Spirit so that, even after times of failure, we will refuse to give up and continue to follow. His heart is that of a lovingly powerful shepherd, and he patiently prods his children to follow persistently, even when we know we haven't followed perfectly.

Have you been wandering? Straying? Do you wonder if your past sin has sidelined you forever? I remind you that Jesus is alive, and he is working powerfully even in the middle of your problems. Why? So that you will see he is who he says he is—Lord and King!—and "return to the Shepherd and Overseer of your soul" (1 Peter 2:25), faithfully believing and fearlessly following.

Tuesday
John 17:3

Wednesday
Philippians 3:8-11

Thursday
Colossians 1:9-12

Friday
Galatians 4:8-9

Saturday/Sunday
Ephesians 3:16-19

"Jesus continually makes himself known to us through his Word and by his Spirit so that, even after times of failure, we will refuse to give up and continue to follow."

WEEK 15
You Already Are One

When it comes to being a witness (Acts 1:8), it's never a matter of "Will you be one?" Rather, it's always a matter of "What kind will you be?"

This is abundantly clear in Acts 1:8, when Jesus said, "But you will receive power when the Holy Spirit has come upon you, and you will be my witnesses in Jerusalem and in all Judea and Samaria, and to the end of the earth."

Notice that when Jesus stated to his disciples that they—and all believers who would eventually follow them—would be filled with the Holy Spirit for the purpose of *being* a witness, he wasn't presenting a suggestion; he was making a declaration. His words are a statement, not a request.

The same conclusion is true in his final words to his disciples on Mount Olivet in what we know as the Great Commission (Matthew 28:16-20). His command to "make disciples of all nations" isn't just one idea in a first-century brainstorming session led by Jesus; it's the only option—the clear command—he left us. Our job isn't to approve it or vote on it. It's to obey it.

That's why, when it comes to Christ's final and parting words, the truest question we can ask ourselves is not, *"Will I be a disciple-making witness?"* but rather, *"What kind of disciple-making witness am I?"*

As you think about that penetrating question today, sensitive to the Holy Spirit's convicting voice, simply consider your next step. Perhaps it is to commit to learning how to succinctly share your testimony. Maybe it means expanding your circle of relationships so that you actually meet more unbelievers. It could be you need to adjust your demeanor so that you're more winsome in your witness. Or possibly you may need to make intentional appointments with your lost friends in order to cross the threshold of opportunity and ask the most important questions.

Whatever your next step, realize it isn't a step towards *agreeing* to be a witness. It's a step towards *accentuating* the witness you already are. For good or bad, you are one. Are you a good one?

What a privilege we have been given—to represent King Jesus, living as an ambassador for him and sharing his worth and weight through our words and actions. Embrace this delightful duty we all share, asking your Heavenly Father to empower you to be the best kind of witness possible for the glory of his name.

Tuesday
Romans 1:16

Wednesday
1 Thessalonians 1:8

Thursday
Acts 4:18-20

Friday
Philippians 2:14-16

Saturday/Sunday
Acts 5:32

"What a privilege to represent King Jesus, living as an ambassador for him and sharing his worth and weight through our words and actions."

WEEK 16
Why the Righteous Are Bold

When you have nothing to hide, you have no reason to run.

Solomon, inspired by the Holy Spirit, clues us in to this truth when he wrote, "The wicked flee when no one pursues, but the righteous are bold as a lion" (Proverbs 28:1). Clearly he understood that sin produces gripping fear, but obedience results in transparent courage.

Let that principle blanket you for a moment: obedience results in transparent courage. And it's not just a principle; it's a promise as well. God assures his children that boldness will flow when obedience is pursued.

Often we switch the order of these two connected elements. We falsely reason, *"Once I feel bold enough, then I'll obey."* People express this backwards equation in regards to things like being baptized, witnessing to a friend, or committing to long-term service as a missionary.

But the reality is boldness comes from obedience, not before it. This is why the righteous are bold: they know their actions are founded upon, and in response to, God and his Word. So they need not fear or worry about the outcome. Righteous people know that obedience isn't about feeling a lack of fear before taking action, but more about the presence of courage in the middle of action.

Yes, righteous people obey and leave the consequences to God. They don't run in fear from what's right. Instead, they run into obedience, unafraid of the unknown, confident God owns it.

The mantra of the righteous isn't what our culture has been touting for over 2 years: *"Stay safe."* No, the clarion call of the righteous, in both word and action, is simply this: *"Stay brave."*

Tuesday
Psalm 27:1

Wednesday
1 Corinthians 16:13

Thursday
2 Corinthians 3:12

Friday
2 Timothy 1:7-8

Saturday/Sunday
Acts 4:31

"God assures his children that boldness will flow when obedience is pursued."

WEEK 17
It's Never Too Late

It's never too late for someone to be rescued from hell.

This must have been what Jude was referencing when, while encouraging believers to show mercy in various ways, he painted the word picture of someone being saved at the last minute. Notice: "Save others by snatching them out of the fire..." (Jude 23).

This is soul-stirring news for those who know someone who has yet to turn to Christ in repentance and faith. After all, with between 70-80% of believers reporting they experienced salvation before the age of 20, it is more than encouraging to know that even if the physical statistics say it is less likely that those who don't yet know Jesus will follow him the older they get, our spiritual hopes can remain high. It's never too late for someone to be rescued from hell.

I witnessed this as a young college student when, while serving as a volunteer youth leader, my youth pastor's father got saved quite literally on his death bed. He had been a devout denier of the gospel, refusing to believe and confess that Jesus Christ lived, died, and rose again. But in his final minutes, he responded to the truth of the gospel in faith, and was miraculously saved by the grace of God just hours before he died. It's never too late for someone to be rescued from hell.

Centuries before that, the thief on the cross experienced the same thing—salvation at the last minute. Hanging on the Roman instrument of death called a cross, the guilty criminal of man realized the he was crucified next to the innocent Lamb of God. And that through his substitutionary death, he could actually be given life. So he believed, confessed, and Jesus, even in his own agony, promised him "today you will be with me in paradise" (Luke 23:43). It's never too late for someone to be rescued from hell.

Keep believing this truth, fellow pilgrim. Those who are getting closer and closer to the gallows of judgment, their feet inching ever nearer to the flames of hell, still may experience mercy, even in the final minutes of their life. God saves the second one believes. It's never too late for someone to be rescued from hell.

And keep sharing this truth, faithful traveler. Always praying, too. Grace can come, even on death row. After all, you were on death row at one point, though perhaps not as close to your final breath as the ones for whom you're praying and with whom you're sharing.

Don't quit believing. Sharing. Praying. Because it's never too late for someone to be rescued from hell.

Tuesday
Romans 10:14-15

Wednesday
Matthew 9:37-38

Thursday
1 Peter 3:15-16

Friday
2 Corinthians 5:17-21

Saturday/Sunday
Matthew 5:16

"Grace can come, even on death row."

WEEK 18
A Final Four

Just 12 words. Four commands. One verse.

That is a numerical summary of 1 Corinthians 16:13, which reads, "Be watchful, stand firm in the faith, act like men, be strong."

With compelling clarity and striking succinctness, Paul is calling for attitudes and actions that enable endurance. What's necessary, the Apostle writes, is emotional, spiritual, and physical strength to persevere and continue.

But why? The verse just before this—16:12—gives us the possible first clue: the Corinthian believers were not going to see Apollos after all. The context indicates they were anxiously anticipating a visit from their fellow brother, perhaps because he would come along side with encouragement and support. But with the news that he was not going to visit them as previously thought, they would, more than ever, need to maintain their commitment to the Lord and one another. So, in light of his absence, do what is necessary to stay vertically and horizontally faithful.

However, the following verse—16:14—gives us the possible second clue: doing everything in love is hard work. The Corinthian believers were facing monumental challenges in their church, such as the selfish misuse of spiritual gifts, personality parties and celebrity-ism, taking advantage of the Lord's Supper, and suing others in court for personal gain. None of these were actions rooted in love for one another. To end carnal behavior would require an immense amount of discipline and strength, the kind that can only come from a vertical and horizontal focus.

That's why verse 13 is so beautifully bold and promising. It is giving us four actions the Corinthians took to ensure that, even when left without the aid of a spiritual shepherd, they would love one another in all they did. It was to this end they were attentive ("be watchful"), convictional ("stand firm in the faith"), courageous ("act like men"), and stalwart ("be strong").

Today, take the necessary actions that lead to winning where it matters—loving one another. This is how the world will know we belong to Jesus, "when we have love for one another."

Tuesday
1 John 4:7-8

Wednesday
Romans 12:10

Thursday
1 Peter 4:8

Friday
1 Thessalonians 4:9

Saturday / Sunday
1 Peter 1:22

"Loving one another is winning where it matters."

WEEK 19
Falling Apart

Someone once truly noted, "A Bible that is falling apart usually belongs to someone who isn't."

I watched this reality in the lives of my mother and father who both had Bibles that were regularly opened, read, and marked in noticeably intriguing ways. Frankly, after even only a few years, each of my parent's Bible always looked like it had been through a battle with a set of red and blue pens and lost.

But what wasn't lost was the impact the Bible had on them.

Don't hear me saying that marking in your Bible is the point. Not at all! The point is the Bible itself. For my parents, opening, reading, and marking in it was—and still is—just their way of showing how much they love and read it; how much they desire to remember and obey it. It's obvious Roger and Betty Stiles are keenly aware God has provided them with a "lamp" and a "light" for every moment and every mile.

I draw this from Psalm 119:105, where David describes God's Word, specifically God's Law, as a "lamp to my feet" and a "light to my path." This is a beautifully practical metaphor upon which one should meditate. Let me explain.

When David connects lamp and feet, he is referring to our next steps; the situations right in front of us in the "right now" moments of life. Aren't you thankful God's Word shows us how to walk and what to do in the immediate things that demand a decision? You can count on God's Word *today*.

The latter couplet of words, light and path, point to how God's Word illuminates the road ahead, providing a "map," of sorts, for our life. Aren't you grateful God already knows where you've yet to go and has left you dependable directions? Though we don't know all the specifics that will come our way, we can be confident God's Word will correctly lay out the path for us, guiding us at every turn mile after mile. You can count on God's Word *tomorrow*.

This is the central habit and core trait of the person whose life isn't falling apart: their Bible usually is.

Though I employ that play on words with a hint of humor, the point it makes should bring us to a serious evaluation of our regular routines and processes: Is God's Word embedded in them? Is Scripture our essential "go to" for the day and our constant compass for the future? Are we into the Word and is the Word into us?

My prayer for you this week is this: Rely on the Bible for every moment and every mile. Read it veraciously. Ingest it deeply. Memorize it patiently. Obey it courageously. Share it widely. Walk in it confidently.

And when your current copy falls apart, take heart. Your life won't.

Tuesday
2 Timothy 3:16-17

Wednesday
Isaiah 40:8

Thursday
Matthew 24:35

Friday
James 1:21

Saturday/Sunday
1 Thessalonians 2:13

"We can be confident God's Word will correctly lay out the path for us, guiding us at every turn mile after mile."

WEEK 20
O-B-E-D-I-E-N-C-E

A firm foundation makes all the difference.

This is precisely the point of the parable Jesus told at the end of his sermon on Mount Olivet (Matthew 7:24-27). He described two people: one who built a house on rock, and one who built a house on sand. Interestingly, other than this initial difference, both are described in very similar ways as "hearing these words of mine" (vs. 24, 26), and then seeing how "the rains fell, the floods came, and the winds blew and beat on that house" (vs. 25, 27).

Frankly, the bulk of the parable concerns how they are alike, except for one distinctive element: one built on rock, and one built on sand. One built on a firm foundation, the other didn't.

A question surfaces: What is the "rock?" What is the firm foundation? What is Jesus communicating in this distinction?

Here's the answer: The importance of obedience to what he says. In fact, he plainly declares this with two all-important phrases. The first one? "...and does them..." (v24). The second? "...and does not do them..." (v. 26)

You see it, don't you? Obedience to Jesus' sayings is the raw material—the "rock"—of a firm foundation for life. Without obedience, you're merely window shopping at the hardware store or lumber yard, acting like you're going to buy the necessary ingredients for your foundation. But if you never actually purchase the right elements, you'll discover, when the storms come and your house doesn't last, that intentions are never as strong as action. Obedience makes all the difference.

James echoes this same principle when he declares we should be "*doers* of the Word, and not hearers only" (James 1:22). And he doubles down on this assertion, saying that if you think just hearing lays a good foundation, you're "deceiving yourself" (v. 22). What an apt description of the person in the parable who built on sand: deceived. Yes, obedience makes all the difference.

Likewise, Jesus affirmed this principle again when, in the Great Commission, he commanded his disciples to "make disciples of all nations...teaching them to *obey* everything I have commanded..." True disciples aren't content with absorbing information; they are bent on obedience, namely, making other disciples who obey everything Jesus commanded. After all, obedience makes all the difference.

If you desire a life that will endure life's storms with incredible stability, begin obeying what Jesus has said. Start today taking action on what the Bible commands. Stop debating and begin doing. Obedience is the way to build a life that won't be torn to shreds by the winds of trials and difficulties. It's what lays a firm foundation for a life that lasts.

Obedience makes all the difference.

Tuesday
John 14:23

Wednesday
Deuteronomy 5:33

Thursday
James 1:22

Friday
Psalm 128:1

Saturday/Sunday
Joshua 1:8

"Obedience to Jesus' sayings is the raw material of a firm foundation for life."

WEEK 21
Not Beyond or Below

Spiritual deception can be dressed up or dressed down. We can be fooled by what's added to the truth or by what's missing from the truth.

John refers to this devilish possibility in his second epistle when he warns his readers about those who "do not remain in Christ's teaching" but "go beyond," as well as the one who does not "bring this teaching" (2 John 9-10). With bold words John gives clear instruction to avoid anyone who adds to the truth or takes away from it. Both are deceitful, decisive, and destructive.

To avoid deception in either direction, we must be dedicated to knowing the truth of God's Word. Believers should prioritize "searching the Scriptures" as the Bereans did (Acts 17:11), and pastors and teachers need to place a high value upon "rightly dividing the Word" as Timothy did (2 Tim 2:15). This means making sure none of us go beyond or below the truth, asserting it means more or less than what it actually means. Whether in exhorted preaching or expected practice, God's Word, not our wishes, sets the table for what we feast on as God's sheep.

Today, use God's Word as the ultimate filter for everything. Whether reading, hearing, singing, or watching, allow Scripture to determine the veracity of everything you take in. And if it's beyond or below the Bible, beware: the bait is on the hook. Don't bite.

Because we can be fooled by what's added or by what's missing.

Tuesday
Isaiah 40:8

Wednesday
Acts 17:11

Thursday
Hebrews 4:12

Friday
1 Thessalonians 2:13

Saturday/Sunday
2 Timothy 3:16-17

"To avoid deception, believers must be dedicated to knowing the truth of God's Word."

WEEK 22
Every 'No' Has a Deeper 'Yes'

Restraint is never as powerful as pursuit.

This doesn't mean we shouldn't say 'no,' resist sin, or, as Jesus said, "deny ourselves" (Matthew 16:24). But it does mean that the discipline to say 'no' when it's needed is fueled by the desire of a deeper 'yes.'

Paul proclaimed exactly this in Philippians 3:10 when he so passionately declared his spiritual aim: "that I may know Christ!" This was his primary pursuit, and it empowered him to resist the pull of things that would have detoured him from God's will. In fact, he alludes to this earlier in the chapter when he writes that he willingly counted all of his pre-Christ success as "rubbish" in order to "gain Christ" (3:8). Essentially, Paul said 'no' to the appeal of worldly approval because of his deeper desire to say 'yes' to a divine relationship.

This principle applies across the board. There's no area where positive pursuit isn't stronger than negative restraint; where a deep 'yes' isn't fueling the necessary 'no.' It's why the overweight person loses the extra pounds—they desire better health more than bigger portions. It's why the distant couple decides to move toward one another, not further away—they want intimacy, not adultery. It's why the father prioritizes his schedule so that family comes before work—he values presence more than presents, a legacy more than regret. Whether it's the student at school, supervisor at work, parent at home, or Christian in the culture, external progress actually stems from an internal pursuit, a decision to value what is truly important, not just what is temporarily appealing. Saying 'no' to those lesser things comes from saying 'yes' to greater things.

Since it applies in all arenas, it is wise to make sure we aren't unintentionally living a spiritual life built only on saying 'no.' At some point that ground will give way; you'll lose your grip and let go of the faith you thought you had out of sheer spiritual fatigue.

How much more biblical to build on the foundation of saying 'yes' to God; to pursuing him who is our single greatest treasure and weightiest source of joy and happiness. How much more deeply satisfying to "press on toward the goal for the prize of the upward call of God in Christ Jesus" (3:14). Pursuing God is where endurance is discovered, perseverance prized, obedience fueled, discipline formed, and conformity to Christ experienced.

Today, let us pursue Christ first so that we resist sin effectively, "counting everything as loss for the surpassing worth of knowing Christ Jesus my Lord" (3:8).

Tuesday
John 17:3

Wednesday
1 John 5:20

Thursday
Colossians 1:9-12

Friday
1 John 2:3

Saturday/Sunday
John 14:21

"Saying 'no' to lesser things comes from saying 'yes' to greater things."

WEEK 23
Long-Distance Eyes

One of the best ways to battle sin in the moment is to think about its consequences in the distance.

This is the heartbeat of a simple phrase in Proverbs 5:11, nine words that form the fateful condition of those who refuse to fight sexual sin: "and at the end of your life you groan."

With stark imagery, Solomon warns us that refusing to listen to God's words and, instead, chasing the enticing temptations of sexual sin will ultimately lead to complete "consummation" (5:11) and "utter ruin" (5:14). There's no fairy tale ending for those who stray from following the Lord; the end destination is "bitter" (5:4), even if the temporary rest stop is sweet.

Pondering sin's ultimate destruction can help us resist its initial deceitfulness. Without a doubt sin always promises more than it can deliver. It is always a mirage; a bait and switch. It thrives on smoke and mirrors. When tempted, tell yourself this truth repeatedly, no matter how luring the lying trap.

The writer of Hebrews penned a similar thought when he recounted Moses' decision to align himself with God's people instead of Pharaoh, reminding us that Moses chose "to be mistreated with the people of God than to enjoy the fleeting pleasures of sin" (11:24). It appears Moses was willing to embrace short-term pain for long-term gain. He considered the endgame of sin, and concluded it wasn't worth the price. He was right, and the Red Sea would echo his decision.

Satan and sin, however, want you to do the opposite. They desire you plunge into seeking short-term gain, all the while knowing that in the end you'll experience long-term pain. That's always what sin leaves; its residue is always an end of life that groans.

As you wage war against sin today, think about your life in 10 years. 20 years. 40 years. What will it be like later if you give in this time? Next time? Every time? Never underestimate the exchange you're making when you sin. Adam's one moment of pleasure has resulted in millennia of pain.

How much better to say 'no' to sinful, partial satisfaction in the immediate for divine, full fulfillment in eternity. Live with long-distance eyes, seeing what assuredly matters most, not just what seemingly matters now.

Tuesday
2 Corinthians 10:4

Wednesday
Psalm 119:11

Thursday
1 Timothy 6:11

Friday
Romans 6:11-12

Saturday/Sunday
James 4:7

"Sin always promises more than it can deliver. So when tempted, tell yourself this truth repeatedly, no matter how luring the lying trap."

WEEK 24
Waiting is a Worthy Response

One of the hardest things to do is wait.

This is especially true in times of injustice, such as when one is suffering for righteousness' sake or enduring persecution. Plainly put, it seems almost impossible to wait for wrongs to be made right.

James leaned in to his readers who were wrestling with this very dilemma with this exhortation: "Be patient, therefore, brothers, until the coming of the Lord" (James 5:7). His audience was watching unfair treatment occur (5:1-6), even experiencing it. It appears there was little they could do to affect change. In the midst of this firestorm, James urges them towards patience (5:8). Yes, towards enduring with an eye to the Lord's return. Essentially, waiting, as difficult as it is, is part of the equation of justice.

The fact that waiting is a worthy response to injustice does not preclude the reality that working for justice is also a proper response. Many Scriptures call us to this exact kind of action, especially Micah 6:8. I believe this is not only a God-given instruction, but a divinely created instinct. It is innate to the human nature, when unfairness and injustice arise, to fight against it. Let's never excuse passivity by calling it patience.

But even the most worthwhile activity won't produce ultimate justice. Frankly, though working for immediate justice is good and proper, there is no guarantee that all will be made right in the here-and-now by our actions. That will only happen when Jesus returns and consummates his kingdom.

That's why waiting is a worthy response. It reminds us, even in our necessary pursuit of immediate justice, that we're not powerful enough to produce it perfectly or ultimately. Only Jesus can do that, and he has promised, when he returns in power and glory, to do exactly that when he "makes all things new" (Revelation 21:5).

That's *what* we're waiting on, and that's *Who* we're waiting for. Ultimate justice from the perfectly just One.

Come quickly, Lord Jesus.

Tuesday
Isaiah 40:31

Wednesday
Proverbs 20:22

Thursday
Psalm 27:13-14

Friday
Lamentations 3:23-24

Saturday/Sunday
Isaiah 30:18

"Waiting reminds us, even in our necessary pursuit of immediate justice, that we're not powerful enough to produce it perfectly or ultimately; only Jesus can do that."

WEEK 25
Our First and Best Action

Prayer is our first and best action.

Admittedly, it's not our only action. But it is, in all situations, our first and best one.

But why? God answers this question for us in Philippians 4 where he, through the Apostle Paul, encourages us with these words: "Don't worry about anything, but in everything, through prayer and petition with thanksgiving, present your requests to God. And the peace of God, which surpasses all understanding, will guard your hearts and minds in Christ Jesus" (vs 6-7).

Prayer is our first and best action because 1) it's how we reject and replace worry, and 2) how we experience the protecting peace of God. While these are two distinct reasons, they are linked divinely as well.

Undoubtedly, prayer helps us fight the temptation to fret by providing us with a much better option: talk to God about it. Then, as we communicate with the Lord about that which makes us anxious, we gain access to the very thing we need in those moments—divine, protecting peace, the kind of peace that keeps out the very thoughts that tempt us to worry. It's supernaturally remarkable how prayer activates God's peace to be the patrolling agent of our heart and mind, posting a "keep out" sign over them aimed directly at Satan and his demons.

Furthermore, I'm delightfully intrigued with the two words *"anything"* and *"everything."* The first word is the umbrella label regarding what we're not to worry about—anything. And the second word? It's the overarching label regarding what we're to pray about—everything. No wonder we consistently affirm the practical principle that, in all situations, prayer is our first and best action. Yes, about anything and in everything.

So today, when you're tempted to stress because of family problems, pray. When you're lured into worrying over a financial crisis, pray. When you're leaning towards fretting over personal failure, pray. When you're facing the valley of a life-altering illness, pray. When you're looking at a mountain of changes you never thought you'd encounter, pray.

Sure, do other things, too. Apologize. Work. Save. Press on. Endure. Persevere.

But by all means, pray. Right away. And keep on praying. It's your first and best action.

Tuesday
Romans 8:26

Wednesday
James 5:16

Thursday
Hebrews 4:16

Friday
Matthew 6:9-13

Saturday/Sunday
Mark 11:24

"Prayer provides us with access to the very thing we need in moments of worry and fret—divine, protecting peace."

WEEK 26
The Fear of Man is a Trap

Fear paralyzes. It cripples. It stalls and halts even the best intentions.

That's why Solomon called it a "snare." Specifically, his words in Proverbs 29:25 are that "the fear of man lays a snare, but whoever trusts in the Lord is safe." God's Word is revealing that fearing man and his opinion of us is actually an enemy of our faith. When we replace faith in God with fear of man, we will find ourselves trapped. In the words of the text, "ensnared," meaning unable to free ourselves from the clutches of another's hold.

The antidote to fearing man is trusting God. This requires two things.

First, we must keep our eyes vertical, looking upwards to Jesus as the standard. He is the Captain of our Salvation, the main character in God's story of redemption. Keeping our eyes fixed on him as our loving Savior and coming Judge will prevent us from wandering, looking around horizontally for others' approval. When our eyes drift from the vertical position, our faith weakens and fear rises. We end up taking detours because of this fear that eventually lead to destruction. Truly, that fear becomes a trap that stops us in our tracks, leaving us vulnerable and victoryless.

Second, we must keep our feet biblical, standing strong on God's Word as the basis for all that we believe and do. God has spoken, and his Word is clear. Our response is to stay put, not shifting away from it due to cultural pressure, political correctness, or personal ease. The minute we look for footing outside of the foundation of Scripture, we're stepping into the snare set by the devil, namely, being caught by the fear of others that keeps you from living with faith in God.

Now, perhaps more than ever, God's people need fixed eyes and settled feet.

Today, when you're tempted to step away from both the Word of God and the Son of God, resist that deceitful, temporarily beautiful, lure. It's an illusion. You may think you're gaining traction with others, but you're really getting trapped by your fear of them.

Live, instead, on the rock of faith in God, not on the sand of the fear of man. Enjoy the lasting security that comes from having your eyes fixed on Jesus and your feet set on his Word.

Tuesday
Isaiah 41:10

Wednesday
John 14:27

Thursday
Psalm 46:1-3

Friday
Hebrews 13:6

Saturday/Sunday
Psalm 56:3-4

"The minute we look for footing outside of the foundation of Scripture, we're stepping into the snare set by the devil."

WEEK 27
The Counter-Cultural Christ

Jesus Christ was the consummate counter-culture communicator.

Consider Matthew 5. Six times he said to the crowds, "You have heard it said...", laying out the current societal norm on various issues. But he followed that up with "But I say unto you...", clarifying the spiritual, eternal truth on those same issues. He repeatedly took aim at what the culture had told them regarding things such as anger, divorce, promises, and retaliation for the purpose of setting a higher standard—His!

There's no getting around it. Jesus dismantled man's wisdom and demonstrated God's. He was the master orator with divine authority. Not once did he worry about man's disapproval or wish for the opposite. Satisfying the culture wasn't his goal. Rather, it was pleasing God.

Ironically, it was in his counter-culture communication about God's standards that he most clearly showed others their need for God's solution, which was himself. Think about it—in relaying God's holy and high expectations regarding the issues of life, everyone who heard him realized they were unable to meet that level of righteousness. It had to be a starkly sobering moment when people who heard him wondered, *"What am I going to do? I'll never measure up."*

That's why I absolutely love the invitation he gives to the crowds just a little further into his ministry, an invitation to "come to me, all who labor and are heavy laden, and I will give you rest. Take my yoke upon you, and learn from me, for I am gentle and lowly in heart, and you will find rest for your souls. For my yoke is easy, and my burden is light." (Matthew 11:28-30). Jesus never left people without hope, even when exposing their hypocrisy in his laser-like teaching. He assured them it wasn't a matter of measuring up, but rather yoking up. And he would be the one in the yoke with them, living his life through them. He was the one who would meet all the requirements for righteousness, and as they were in the yoke with him, they would experience the blessings and benefits of his perfect yoke-bearing. He would do the work, which is why the yoke was easy and the burden was light.

That same promise holds true today for anyone who believes and follows Jesus. At the end of your "It's never good enough" rope is the hope of Christ's "It is finished" work. Supernaturally, he will live his life through you, positioning you in himself so that you quit trying harder and start trusting happily. When that occurs, his commandments are not burdensome, but rather a blessing (1 John 5:3). They simply become the avenue through which we display loving obedience to God, not a ladder of accomplishments we're trying to climb to impress him. That's a counter-culture life!

If the sound of this cuts against the grain, if it sounds like the opposite of what you normally hear from the world, don't be surprised. That's exactly what Jesus does—counters the culture so that people encounter God. And it's that very counter-cultural Word that proves to be the soul-saving message and life-changing truth we need.

Tuesday
Revelation 3:20

Wednesday
Isaiah 1:18

Thursday
James 2:5

Friday
Matthew 6:33

Saturday/Sunday
Matthew 7:13-14

"At the end of your 'It's never good enough' rope is the hope of Christ's 'It is finished' work."

WEEK 28
Living or Limiting?

Obedience doesn't limit the believer. It actually enables the believer to truly live.

This is the heartbeat of Proverbs 7:2, where Solomon exhorts his son to "keep my commandments and live." This simple statement, which opens the chapter, is set against the solemn warning that closes the chapter, an alarm concerning the "forbidden woman" and "adulteress." That warning? "Her house is the way to Sheol, going down to the chambers of death" (7:27).

What's positioned between the opening words of life and the closing words of death? The call to obedience. With the starkest of language, Solomon shows the deathly danger that awaits those who refuse to resist sexual temptation and provides ample motivation to stay far away from the cliff of uncontrolled lusts. He elevates the beauty of obedience, prioritizing it as the avenue to truly enjoying life.

The world, the flesh and the devil would have you believe otherwise. This trifecta of evil deceitfully claims that unbridled passion has no consequences. They seductively yet falsely assert that you should do what do what is right in your own eyes. What they fail to reveal is that "sin, when it is finished, brings forth death" (James 1:15), and the end results of doing your own thing "are the ways of death" (Proverbs 14:12).

No wonder Solomon lifted up obedience as the doorway to life. He desired deeply for his sons to follow the Law of the Lord. He knew their obedience to God wouldn't limit their life, but would, instead, enable them to experience true life. Thus, he called for them on multiple occasions to "let your heart keep my commandments, for length of days and years of life they will add to you" (3:1-2), "hear, my son, and accept my words that the years of your life may be many" (Proverbs 4:10), and "be attentive to my words...for they are life" (Proverbs 4:20).

Today, commit to obeying Jesus. Decide to follow the God's Word. Submit to the authority of Scripture. It isn't limiting you at all. It is actually sparing you from death and leading you to true life.

Tuesday
1 John 5:3

Wednesday
Jeremiah 7:23

Thursday
John 8:51

Friday
1 John 3:24

Saturday/Sunday
Joshua 24:15

"The beauty of obedience is in the fact that it is the avenue to truly enjoying life."

WEEK 29
Two Take-Aways After a Year in the Prophets

Julie and I spent the bulk of our 2021 Bible reading in the Old Testament books of prophecy. Each night we'd take some time together and read an assigned portion from one of the minor or major prophets, eventually working our way through all of them by the end of the year. It was an invigorating spiritual journey for us as a couple and as individuals.

Neither of us would pretend it was always easy to understand. Elements of Ezekiel left us wide-eyed, aspects of Amos puzzled and amazed us, and specific questions in Malachi moved us to memorable moments of deeper faith in God and fear of God. Yet, in every passage we read from the prophets, two truths consistently emerged that have left an indelible mark on me.

1. *God is indescribably patient.* The prophets were God's messengers to Israel, warning them of coming judgment and calling them to immediate repentance. To be sure, God sent prophet after prophet after prophet, a long line of voices urging them to return to him, their loving Father. In fact, God's compassionate voice was heard and his loving arms were extended for over 450 years! Even during their 70 years of captivity, which was their punishment for centuries of idolatry, God assured them he would revive them if they'd return to him. Plainly put, there's no way to read the prophets without seeing the long arm of the Lord and the patient posture of the Father.

2. *God is sovereignly powerful.* Though he spoke through his prophets, God worked through a number of different things to alert his people to their need to return. Pagan nations,

unbelieving kings, immoral people, tragic circumstances, natural disasters, and life events were all elements God used to both illuminate and illustrate to his people their waywardness and rebellion. Nothing was outside of his control or command. There's simply no way to read the prophets without seeing the mighty hand of God orchestrating all things for his purposes.

The good news is this — God hasn't changed. He is still both of these: *indescribably patient* and *sovereignly powerful*. He loves beyond description and moves without permission. He desires all people everywhere to repent so that is glory is maximized in the lives of his creation. And he's not only communicating that message through his Word and witnesses, he's ordaining all other things for these reasons as well. All creation points to God's glory and man's need to worship him, and it cries out to be heard. Yes, both verbally and visually, God is sending the message to us still that he is patiently waiting (2 Peter 3:9) and powerfully working (Romans 16:25-27).

Today, harden your heart no longer. Stop stiffening your neck. Open your ears to hear the Lord's plea to return to him. Look around you at all the ways he is still, time and time again, reaching out to you. And run to the Father, the eternal God who is indescribably patient and sovereignly powerful.

Tuesday
Jeremiah 10:6

Wednesday
Jude 1:24-25

Thursday
Psalm 95:3

Friday
1 Timothy 6:16

Saturday/Sunday
Job 37:5

"God is sending the message to us still that he is patiently waiting and powerfully working."

WEEK 30
A Command and a Promise

I contend and believe the Great Commission is both a *command* to be obeyed and a *promise* that has been fulfilled.

Perhaps you're wondering, "What is the Great Commission?" It is the final words of Jesus as recorded by Matthew in chapter 28 — "Go, therefore, and make disciples of all nations, baptizing them in the name of the Father and of the Son and of the Holy Spirit, teaching them to observe everything I have commanded you. And remember, I am with you always, to the end of the age."

My contention that this is both a command and a promise brings up an obvious question: "If it has been fulfilled, why obey it?" It's one worth answering for sure.

I believe the *command* of the Great Commission relates to its theological effect, and the *promise* of the Great Commission relates to its eschatological effect. And our obedience is connected to both. Let me explain starting with the latter first.

Several biblical texts indicate Jesus' return (i.e., a final aspect of the end) is predicated upon the gospel being preached to all nations. Yet, throughout the letters to the churches of the first century, Christ's return was considered imminent, or as one author said, "impending." Frankly, it is hard to read any of the epistles and not sense that the apostles were expecting Christ to return soon, even within their lifetime. Some see a shift in Paul's emphasis in his later letters, but the fact remains that, with rare exception, the early church's leaders lived in anticipation of this next event on God's agenda.

So we must ask ourselves—why would they live with such eager anticipation if there was doubt about the one thing Jesus himself said would be the initiating event? It's because they knew it had occurred. They were confident that, eschatologically, nothing needed to happen for Jesus to return. He had ascended, the Spirit had descended, the gospel had been preached to all nations, and the end (or last days) were now initiated. So longing and looking for their Lord's return was their natural response as they were going about making disciples. So the assurance of his soon return, based on the fulfilled promise of the Great Commission, enabled hope-filled obedience to Jesus' words in their difficult days.

Essentially, the Great Commission as a promise was fulfilled in order to assure them—and us—that nothing else needs to happen in order for Jesus to return. This is not to say there aren't signs of his return, but rather that there aren't *stop* signs. However hard their circumstances, they could take joy in this fact: Jesus was coming back. His return was— and is—next!

As a command, however, the Great Commission calls for obedience. Why? Because of its theological effect, namely, that God actually still does now what he did then—saves sinners from every ethnicity through the preaching of the gospel. He does this through the ordained means of disciple making, that process of a person believing the gospel, being baptized, then instructed how to obey what Jesus said (which, in turn, means they, too, will make disciples). It is because God is who he says he is and does what he says he will do that we continue in the pattern of the first disciples and obey the command of spiritual reproduction without ethnic distinction. We do this, not to bring about the end, but precisely because it is the end.

Remember, this fulfilled promise does not mean we don't continue to obey Jesus' final instructions with the globe fully in view. It simply means we don't do so with the pressure to complete it so that he can return. This is, essentially, the theological effect of the Great Commission: joyful obedience to our great God who saves without distinction.

This promise and command—the Great Commission—is the overarching task of the church and perfectly blends her eschatology, theology, and missiology. It is our overarching task, not because we have to finish it, but because we desire to be faithful to it. We don't make disciples to leverage Christ's return, but because we long for Christ's return. This is fundamental to what we believe about the mission of the church and missions in the church.

Today and this week, live as a joyful, expectant disciplemaker, looking both upward and outward. Let's long for our Lord's coming even while we love our neighbor, praying daily, "Come quickly, Lord Jesus."

Tuesday
Romans 10:14-15

Wednesday
John 1:45

Thursday
Matthew 4:19-20

Friday
Revelation 7:9

Saturday/Sunday
Isaiah 6:8

"The Great Commission is the overarching task of the church and perfectly blends her eschatology, theology, and missiology."

WEEK 31
The Strange Ways of God

God's conviction comes in different ways. Odd ways even. Yet all of them accomplish their purpose: to expose our sin and turn us back to him.

Such was the case for Jonah.

Nineveh had just experienced revival, and Jonah was outside the city angrily and jealously conversing with God about exactly that: Nineveh's revival. He knew God would be gracious in response to their repentance, and it bothered him that God would show mercy and forgive. So he constructed a small tent for himself and asked God to take his life (Jonah 4:1-4).

Instead, God saved his life.

God ordained three things to turn Jonah's perspective around and rescue him physically: a plant, a worm, and wind. The plant actually shielded him from the sun during his pity-party, until the worm overcame the plant the next day. As soon as the plant withered, a scorching wind came and "beat down on the head of Jonah" (Jonah 4:8). Jonah found himself angry once more, but this time over the fate of the plant. And his own! So he requested once again to die (Jonah 4:9).

It was in the middle of this arrogant self-pity that God showed Jonah the irony of his anger through a penetrating question. It's recorded in Jonah 4:10-11. Here's the gist of it—*You're upset about the withering of a plant because it was your shade, yet you were wishing I would have destroyed over 120,000 people? Really Jonah? What's up with that?*

Interestingly, that's how the 4-chapter book ends—with that staggeringly convicting question from God. And no answer is recorded. Talk about a cliff hanger.

We don't know what happened next; we can only surmise. My opinion? I think Jonah repented of his pride and prejudice and returned to the Lord. I think that because when previously convicted by another strangely sovereign circumstance—being swallowed by a big fish—his response was repentance. I personally believe he did the same thing again after considering the plant. And the worm. And the wind.

Ah, the plant and the worm and the wind. Three unlikely things sent by God to expose Jonah's sin and turn him back to God. No doubt a strange way to work in Jonah's life. But strangely effective.

Such is God's sovereign control and steadfast love. Nothing is outside of his control and no one is outside of his reach.

Not a plant. Not a worm. Not the wind. And not Jonah.

Tuesday
Isaiah 45:7-9

Wednesday
Colossians 1:16-17

Thursday
Proverbs 16:33

Friday
Lamentations 3:37-39

Saturday/Sunday
Job 42:2

"God's sovereign control and steadfast love means nothing is outside of his control and no one is outside of his reach."

WEEK 32
My Old Bible

One of the best habits a person can practice is the regular reading of the Bible.

Scripturally, this often overlooked yet profoundly needed principle is blatantly evident. It is seen throughout Psalm 119, as well as in 2 Timothy 3:16-17, Hebrews 4:12, and 1 Thessalonians 2:13, to name a few.

But I especially like what God said in Joshua 1:8 when he reminded Israel's new leader, "This Book of the Law shall not depart from your mouth, but you shall meditate on it day and night, so that you may be careful to do according to all that is written in it. For then you will make your way prosperous, and then you will have good success."

Or how David described the blessed person in Psalm 1—he said that person's "delight is in the law of the Lord, and on his law he meditates day and night."

Anecdotally, this biblical principle was a constant focus of the church in which I grew up. In multiple ways, the atmosphere was always focused on God's Word, and reading the Bible daily was the normal expectation for every single member. And rightly so! It was a spiritual family where Scripture held a high priority, and I'm deeply grateful for that.

In fact, for a couple of years during my college experience, our new pastor quoted a specific poem about the Bible before every single message. Yes, the same poem every week before every sermon! But it made a difference, because I remember specific lines, as well as the main point, of that poem to this day. I can even now, even while I'm writing this, hear his unique cadence and inflection as I rehearse the stanzas of the poem.

That poem? I thought you'd never ask.

My Old Bible

Though the cover is worn,
And the pages are torn,
And though places bear traces of tears,
Yet more precious than gold
Is this Book worn and old,
That can shatter and scatter my fears.

This old Book is my guide,
'Tis a friend by my side,
It will lighten and brighten my way;
And each promise I find
Soothes and gladdens the mind,
As I read it and heed it each day.

To this Book I will cling,
Of its worth I will sing,
Though great losses and crosses be mine;
For I cannot despair,
Though surrounded by care,
While possessing this blessing Divine.

(Author unknown)

Before your close your eyes in sleep tonight, take intentional time to read your Bible. Feast on God's Word. Devour the Scriptures. It will be one of the best things you'll do today that will affect all of your tomorrows.

Tuesday
Romans 15:4

Wednesday
Isaiah 55:11

Thursday
Luke 24:27

Friday
2 Peter 1:19-21

Saturday/Sunday
Psalm 119:105

"One of the best habits a person can practice is the regular reading of the Bible."

WEEK 33
The Clear Will of God

God doesn't play hide or seek with his children. He's not obscuring his plan; he doesn't communicate in cryptic fashion. No, God reveals his will plainly. He has made it known.

In fact, God is so committed to clarity regarding his will that he inspired Paul, in 1 Thessalonians 5:16-18, to identify three things in exactly that way—as God's will. Notice this one sentence (3 short verses): "Rejoice always, pray without ceasing, give thanks in all circumstances, for this is the will of God in Christ Jesus concerning you."

If you've ever wondered, *"What's God's will for me?"*, these verses give us at least three items that should answer that question: Rejoicing, prayer, and thankfulness. There's no ambiguity whatsoever; it's ultra-plain and Windex-clear.

Specifically, consider these definitions:

- Rejoicing – gladness and delight
- Prayer – approaching God with praise, intercessions, requests.
- Thankfulness – expressions of gratefulness and appreciation

When there's this kind of clarity, our obedience should be quick. Without hesitation. After all, no analysis is needed. God's expectations are front and center. He has shown us lucidly what he "wills" for his children. Thus, we should respond promptly.

Today, live in the very center of God's will by exulting in God, praying to God, and thanking God. Experience the joy of proving what is the will of God (Romans 12:2) by engaging in these actions.

For sure, there's nothing vague or murky about this. It's the clear will of God.

Tuesday
1 Timothy 2:1-4

Wednesday
Hebrews 13:20-21

Thursday
1 Thessalonians 4:3

Friday
1 Peter 2:15

Saturday/Sunday
Hebrews 10:36

"God's expectations are front and center. He has shown us lucidly what he 'wills' for his children."

WEEK 34
Just Ask the Birds

God is not distant or unreachable. He is not remote or unaware. He is, instead, close. Personal. Near. Concerned.

This is precisely what Jesus was communicating to his disciples when he illustrated God's intimate knowledge of and care for them by talking about birds and flowers (Matthew 6:26-30). He succinctly stated that "your Heavenly Father feeds them [the birds]" and then rhetorically asked, "Are you not of more value than they?" The answer? Of course you are!

When telling them to consider the flowers of the field and how God dresses them so beautifully and faithfully, he again rhetorically asked, "If God so clothes the grass of the field...will he not much more clothe you...?" The answer? Of course he will!

Jesus ends his simple, down-to-earth illustration with this comforting assertion, "Your heavenly Father knows..." (6:32). What a powerful promise on which to stand: God knows!

I find it amazing that things as simple as sparrows and lilies were used by Jesus to teach us such deep things about God. Specifically, that God is close, concerned, aware, and responsive. He is near, attentive, dependable, and intimate. These words describe why we are theists and believe God has a personal relationship to his creatures.

Jesus' teaching also forms the basis for why we are *not* deists, the false understanding that God does not intervene in the affairs of his creatures nor is he interested in interacting with them. While one could show this to be untrue through theological argument and debate, I like the way Jesus clarified it: through simple analogy and pictures.

If you've ever wondered if God knows, if he cares, if he acts, if he is moved, take a look outside. Nature overwhelmingly tell us God does know. He does care. He does act. He is moved. He is the one God who has made everything, and the one God who relates to it all perfectly. Intimately. Personally.

Yes, God is one and he knows each one of his children.

Just ask the birds.

Tuesday
Psalm 55:22

Wednesday
Philippians 4:19

Thursday
Deuteronomy 31:8

Friday
Matthew 10:29-31

Saturday/Sunday
Isaiah 46:4

"God is close, concerned, aware, and responsive. He is near, attentive, dependable, and intimate."

WEEK 35
A Divine Equation

Genuine desire evidenced by gritty diligence results in godly growth.

Solomon showcases this principle in Proverbs 2 through two words: "if" and "then." Three times he uses "if" (2:1, 3, 4), and two times he uses "then" (2:5, 9), with an additional two "so's" that serve a then-like function.

Through the word "if," Solomon is calling for desire and diligence in relation to God's wisdom and understanding. He applies several metaphors and word images to the concept of desire and diligence, such as "treasuring up my commandments," "making your ear attentive," "inclining your heart," "raising your voice," as well as "searching for treasure" and "seeking silver."

When it comes to the effect of such a posture and passion, Solomon employs even more descriptive and picturesque language to indicate what awaits the one who is diligent because of their inner desire. He assures they will "understand the fear of the Lord," "find the knowledge of God," "wisdom will come into your heart," "knowledge will be pleasant to your soul," and "discretion will watch over you." And that's not all—in the latter portion of the chapter he lays out the incredible protections that are afforded to the one who prioritizes his or her pursuits to seek the Lord first and foremost.

Proverbs 2 is a classic "if/then" divine equation, showing that deep appetites and diligent actions produce definitive blessings; that genuine desire evidenced by gritty diligence results in godly growth.

But it all starts with the desire. It's our affections that must be stirred if we are going to be motivated to action that results in growth. That's why Solomon began the chapter with the all-important "if." He knew, at the root of it all, was the issue of thirst.

How's your thirst for God? What's your level of desire for spiritual things? How intense are your inner appetites for the divine? Without a doubt your spiritual progress is connected to your spiritual action, but your spiritual action is dependent upon your spiritual affections.

Over the next two weeks we are going to be sharing ways we can increase our spiritual thirst; ways we can awaken, even deepen, our affections for Christ. Today, however, simply rest in this divine equation: *If* you'll focus on asking God to increase your affections for him, *then* you'll find the fuel to act in the necessary ways that will result in deeper growth with him.

Tuesday
Matthew 5:6

Wednesday
Jeremiah 29:13

Thursday
John 6:35

Friday
Psalm 42:1-2

Saturday/Sunday
John 4:13-14

"Spiritual progress is connected to spiritual action, and spiritual action is dependent upon spiritual affections."

WEEK 36
Inner Regeneration

You can't revive what isn't already alive.

So when it comes to deepening one's affections for Christ, a first and foremost question to ask yourself is this: *Do I actually have spiritual affections for Christ? Has the Spirit of God birthed spiritual life in me, giving me a divine nature and new set of appetites?*

Jesus declared to Nicodemus that unless we are "born again," we "cannot see the kingdom of God" (John 3:3), indicating that spiritual sight is impossible apart from the work of God in us. Peter wrote that it is only through God's divine power that we've been given everything we need for life and godliness (2 Peter 1:3), reminding us that it starts, continues, and ends with God's work in us.

This is why, even in broadening our understanding of how to deepen our spiritual affections for Christ, we must quickly embrace this reality: we can't invent them; we can only increase them. Only God gives them, and he does so at the moment of spiritual regeneration—that moment when one is saved by God's grace.

It is futile to expend energy trying to "work up" feelings that have no spiritual roots or basis. It only leads to pretending, playing the game of looking good on the outside with no real substance on the inside.

When one is genuinely born again, however, there isn't a manufacturing of affections for Christ. Instead, there is an increasing awareness of Spirit-birthed, God-given, Christ-focused affections. And as that awareness grows, we willingly, though often slowly, make whatever adjustments we need to make because of the surpassing value of "knowing Christ Jesus" (Phil. 3).

Keep in mind that affections refer to far more than what you do. The concept even dives deeper than knowing you want to do what you do. It goes to why you want to do what you do. This is the essence of affections: *Why* is there a desire to do the deeds you do? *Why* is there a 'want' for the 'what?' The answer? God. And only God.

If there's no desire for the things of God, no thirst for the treasure of Jesus, no motivation to pursue holiness, then the first step *isn't* to "stir the pot" of your heart and hope that you can drum up some kind of spiritual fervor. Not at all! The first step is to ask God to give you his appetites; to grant you his divine nature. The necessary next move is to ask God to save you!

If in this moment you are realizing your true need is authentic salvation, humbly admit you are a sinner who has broken God's law and stand in need of the mercy and grace that comes through the life, death, and resurrection of Jesus (Romans 3:10; 6:23). Believe solely that only through this good news—the gospel—is one saved, and call out in repentance and faith, asking God to forgive you through the Lord Jesus Christ (Romans 10:9, 10, 13). This is the core essence of conversion—taking our stand exclusively on the gospel of God as the only means by which we are made right with God (1 Cor. 15:1-4).

This is the moment everything changes (2 Cor. 5:17). Slowly but surely we are awakened to new appetites, desires, and longings, ones from God through the Holy Spirit. Without a doubt salvation by Christ is the first and foremost necessary ingredient to experiencing affections for Christ.

Tuesday
Ephesians 2:4-5

Wednesday
1 Peter 1:3-4

Thursday
Ezekiel 11:19-20

Friday
John 3:3

Saturday/Sunday
John 1:12-13

"In understanding how to deepen our spiritual affections for Christ, we must quickly embrace this reality: we can't invent them; we can only increase them."

WEEK 37
Vertical Concentration

An old adage warns us not to be so heavenly minded that we're of no earthly good. But that's a false proposition. Frankly, it's precisely the opposite—we think too little about heavenly things. As a result, we often do less good than we should.

This is the core command of Colossians 3:1-2, where Paul beautifully exhorts us to "seek the things that are above" and to "set your mind on things that are above." Without any ambiguity, the call is to live with vertical concentration. A heavenward gaze. A settled view towards our eternal home. This type of thinking—vertical concentration—is a key way believers deepen their affections for Christ.

Why? Because, generally and eventually, our feelings follow our focus. Thus, when our thoughts are intentionally set on Christ and heaven, our emotions and behavior will ultimately be impacted, and we will begin to "feel" and "do" what we "know." When we "seek" and "set," we will start seeing both our desires and deeds change.

In fact, this is how the next section of Colossians 3 unfolds. Paul follows his exhortation to live with vertical concentration by showing the result: horizontal sanctification. Specifically, we begin to experience the transforming power of God to put off the old self (vs 5-11) and put on the new one (vs 12-17). He even concludes with an umbrella-like statement, reminding his fellow believers that whatever they do, whether in word or deed, to "do everything in the name of the Lord Jesus" (v 17). Now that's vertical concentration!

Nestled within this portion of Scripture are two threads I don't want you to miss; common go-to themes that will help us "seek" and "set" so that our affections for Christ are strengthened. Those threads are 1) God's Word and 2) gratefulness.

I'll be the first to admit you can mine much more out of this text. But you dare not miss these two elements at the least. For without a doubt, God's Word and a grateful spirit are essential building blocks to developing a life of vertical concentration. Scripture stands as our solely sufficient source for "learning Christ" (Ephesians 4:20), the One on whom our eyes should be fixed (Hebrews 12:1-2). And thankfulness in all things based on the sovereignty of God over all things enables us to get through all things because we see them from a different perspective—a divinely vertical one. So let each day be drenched with God's Word and a grateful heart.

As you engage in these two central components of vertical concentration, you'll discover your longings and affections for Christ deepening. You'll experience a focus that is increasingly heavenly, a mind gradually becoming more and more occupied and satisfied—renewed—with the treasure of Christ and dissatisfied with the trappings of this world.

So look up, my brother or sister. Settle your sights on the loveliness of our Lord. Cast your eyes to the kingdom of God. This is the kind of vertical concentration that feeds our inner affections.

Tuesday
Jeremiah 29:13

Wednesday
Hebrews 3:1

Thursday
Isaiah 26:3

Friday
Philippians 3:13-14

Saturday/Sunday
Psalm 119:6

"Generally and eventually, our feelings follow our focus."

WEEK 38
Greatly Loved

God does what he does because of who he is. His character always informs his actions.

Not only does this mean God operates fully and eternally in perfect and righteous ways, but it further means God isn't leveraged or manipulated by outside forces. This does not mean God isn't moved or touched by our condition. Rather, that because our condition and situation is known by God, and because he is who he is, he responds to us on the basis of his own essence, not on the basis of our exertion.

This is clearly seen in many Scriptures, where we are told God moves and acts on our behalf out of his own character, not because of our conduct. Notice just a few of the more obvious ones and let them warm your heart for a moment:

> But God, being rich in mercy, because of the great love with which he loved us, even when we were dead in our trespasses, made us alive together with Christ—by grace you have been saved." (Ephesians 2:4-5)
> "For God so loved the world, that he gave his only Son, that whoever believes in him should not perish but have eternal life." (John 3:16)
> "But God shows his love for us in that while we were still sinners, Christ died for us." (Romans 5:8)

A more obscure reference to this same theological truth is found in Daniel. In fact, three times we see the phrase "you are greatly loved" (9:23, 10:11, 10:23), indicating that each time God gifted Daniel with divine insight into visions and mysteries, it wasn't due to anything Daniel did. Instead, it was solely because of God's great affection for Daniel.

How reassuring and comforting to know that God bestows his blessings on us because he has made us his beloved. That's right—the action is all God's from start to finish. Whatever gifts and good we receive, it is due to the lavish grace of God.

Rejoice today, my fellow recipient of God's undeserved yet displayed kindness, that "every good and perfect gift comes from the Father above" (James 1:17), and live in light of the unconditional love and favor of our Lord. Yes, you, too, are greatly loved!

Tuesday
Zephaniah 3:17

Wednesday
Galatians 2:20

Thursday
Psalm 86:15

Friday
Romans 8:38-39

Saturday/Sunday
John 15:9

"Whatever gifts and good we receive, it is due to the lavish grace of God."

WEEK 39
The Truth About Trials

No one likes troubles or trials; yet, everyone has their share of them. No one ever asks for them; still, they raise their ugly head. They are usually unexpected, often undeserved, yet not uncommon.

Joseph, Jacob's favorite son, was no exception to this rule. It seems like he went from the frying pan into the fire and back into the frying pan. Even a quick glance at Genesis reveals Joseph going from one trial to the next.

But, after a deeper look, we see that Joseph's circumstances, though troubling, were all part of God's plan. How can God use a ruined reputation, a crushed dream, a broken heart? Let's find out.

In Genesis 37 Joseph was faced with a *dangerous situation*: he was about to be killed by his brothers by being thrown into a waterless pit. Would this be the end? Suddenly, all of his human security was gone. His future, his health, and his life were at stake.

But Joseph's trip to the pit simply gave God the opportunity to miraculously bring him out by providing a band of Ishmaelites to take him into Egypt. Truly, what we consider our insecurities, God considers His opportunities. Though Joseph had no idea where he was, God did. Remember, God's plan has nothing to do with *location*, for God knows *where* we are even when we don't.

In Genesis 39 we see Joseph faced with a *damaging accusation*: he was accused of rape. Although untrue, rumors spread and

Joseph found himself counting the days behind bars. Although undeserved, Joseph accepted his punishment and said nothing.

How can God work through a ruined testimony? Take heart—what man may say is not what God knows. And God sees our integrity and character while man simply sees our supposed reputation. Remember, God's plan has nothing to do with *reputation*. He knows *what* we are even when others don't.

Finally, in Genesis 41, the truth is revealed and the Egyptians realize Joseph was not a rapist, a coward, or a thief; rather, he was "discreet and wise in all things" (41:39). Joseph is rewarded with *divine vindication*. Though Joseph was still grasping the reason for his trials, he knew God had them planned all along. Truly, the trouble that came to Joseph was used to position him for his higher and more nobler place of responsibility for the sake of God's people. Remember, God's plan has everything to do with *preparation*, and he knows *what is ahead* even when we don't!

Perhaps you think you have taken a wrong turn; maybe you wonder if God really knows you're alive. You ask yourself, "Does God know about my unexpected trip to the hospital next week? Did God hear about my father and his sudden battle with cancer? Is God aware that my wayward child just left home and ran away? Does God care that I seem lost, confused, hurt and broken?"

Yes, He sure does! For He knows where you are even when you don't; He knows what you are even when others don't; and He knows what lies ahead before it ever arrives.

Be encouraged child of God. The Father's plan for your life is not concerned with location or reputation, but rather with preparation. So don't be too anxious to exit your sorrows; sit and learn in the school of hard knocks, for God is the master teacher, and he is fitting you with everything necessary to accomplish his designed will for your life.

Tuesday
1 Peter 5:10

Wednesday
John 16:33

Thursday
Romans 8:18

Friday
Psalm 23:4

Saturday/Sunday
2 Corinthians 12:9

"What we consider our insecurities, God considers His opportunities."

WEEK 40
Weep Not For Me

For the Christian, death is the doorway to the truest life one could ever know.

Paul declared this truth beautifully in 2 Corinthians 5:4, and it has been echoed by many in both song and sermon. They are undoubtedly accurate.

But they always resonate more fully when you're on the steps of that doorway. Admittedly, they don't become more accurate; one simply becomes more acutely aware of their truthfulness when you're on the front porch of that human reality we know as death's doorway.

In light of several of our sheep who have stared at that doorway recently with a loved one, I wanted to share a poem I wrote a couple of years ago. It originated from my time in God's Word one week, and culminated days after Julie's father went to his heavenly home.

May this poetic meditation be another echo of the promise God has given us in times of death and sorrow—we grieve, but with hope (1 Thess. 4:13).

Weep Not For Me

Weep not for me, weep for yourselves
You who still linger here;
I'm finally home, not merely near,
Why mourn for me with tears?

You pilgrims traveling yet on earth,
For you, your tears are shed;

For I no longer wait or wish,
Or battle doubt and fear.

It's true—my eyes were growing dim,
My lungs were gasping deep;
My back was bent, my heart was weak,
At last, I went to sleep.

But death was not arresting me,
Nor was it grimly reaping.
True life was overtaking me,
Why sit you there still weeping?

You now behold my former shell,
My tent that faded fast;
But my mere mortal, passing days
Gave way to what will last.

Ah, "last"—that's where eternity
Rolls on like endless waves;
God's glory as the centerpiece,
Our tongues in ceaseless praise.

So mourn not for my journey there,
It's where I long to be.
His presence is my fullest joy,
So please, don't weep for me.

Instead, weep for the exiles here,
The strangers plodding 'long.
The ones enduring, by God's grace,
Sin's presence, evil's wrong.

It's they who need your mourning cries,
Your sorrow and your prayers.
Not me, for I'm inheriting
God's riches as an heir.

I ran my race, I fought my fight,
My ordained days are done.
Now God has borne me to his home,
Through Christ, the Risen One.

That's why I urge you not to weep
For me, I'm not in need.
But rather weep for you and yours,
Who have yet to be freed

From all you know as toil and strain,
And from its final blow;
You're body-bound until that day
It wears a dusty glow.

But death, with all its weakened wails,
And empty, hollow sting,
Could not shut tight the grave that held
my Savior, Jesus—King!

His resurrection led the way,
believers follow suit:
Because he rose, then so will I,
Because he lives, I, too!

Thus weep for you, weep not for me,
I'm more alive than ever!
I'll see you, saints, when Christ returns,
And then we'll be together.

Tuesday
John 14:1-3

Wednesday
Revelation 21:3

Thursday
Hebrews 13:14

Friday
1 Corinthians 15:51-52

Saturday/Sunday
2 Corinthians 5:1

"For the Christian, death is the doorway to the truest life one could ever know."

WEEK 41
Running From Victory, Not For It

As I watched the Olympics one year, I was intrigued by the sheer motivation many athletes found in striving for a gold medal. Whether swimming or running, wrestling or volleyball, gymnastics or tennis, when the medals were in view, the opportunity to win the gold often spurred them on to an incredible performance, many times even a new Olympic or world record. There's something about "running for a victory" (my generic phrase for competing) that is compellingly motivating.

Except for the Christian. Frankly, we don't run *for* victory at all. We run *from* it.

What do I mean? Well, I don't mean we run *away* from it; that would be silly. I mean we run *because* of it. In other words, we don't run this spiritual race to *achieve* a victory. We run this spiritual race because we have already *received* a victory—Christ's!

This is the essence of the exhortation in Hebrews 12:1-2, where we commanded to "run with endurance the race that is set before us." But we don't run this race in this way to win something; we run this race in this way because Jesus already won something—victory over sin, death, hell, and the grave. He has already conquered the enemy! That's why verse 2 closes with the undeniable reality that Jesus "is seated at the right hand of the throne of God."

That's right, brother or sister, Jesus has already won our victory at the cross. And so we run. And, most assuredly, we run with all our might. In no uncertain terms we run with discipline and diligence (1 Cor 9:24-27). But our motivation to run this spiritual race is not rooted in something we hope to earn in the future. Our running is rooted in what has already occurred in the past—Jesus' victory at Calvary! We don't run for a victory; we run from one.

May you today think about Christ's victorious work at the cross and the grave and consequently find new resolve and strength to run like you've never run before. Patiently. Perseveringly. Productively. Powerfully. May your spiritual running be supernaturally propelled, not because you're looking at what you will get when you finish, but rather because you're remembering what Christ won when he said, "It is finished."

That's why we run. And that's how we run. Not for victory, but from it.

Tuesday
Galatians 6:9

Wednesday
2 Corinthians 3:4-5

Thursday
Philippians 1:6

Friday
2 Corinthians 5:14-15

Saturday/Sunday
Hebrews 12:1

"Our motivation to run this spiritual race is not rooted in something we hope to earn in the future. Our running is rooted in what has already occurred in the past—Jesus' victory at Calvary!"

WEEK 42
God's Incredible Commitment to His People

God rightfully and jealously desires to know his people and be known by his people. And he will do everything to ensure that occurs.

Ezekiel is the proof of the previous statement. In fact, one of the recurring statements in this Old Testament book, especially the first half, is, "Then you will know that I am the LORD." It is a statement of result; one of intention. It is a prominent theme no doubt. Clearly all that Ezekiel was divinely called to portray in his life and proclaim with his lips was aimed at God being known by his people and knowing his people.

What's so striking about this is that Ezekiel is a book largely focused on judgment. It describes not only God's discipline of Israel, but also his punishment of other nations. And in almost every case, the phrase "then you will know that I am the LORD" is the closing refrain. In other words, God was bringing his people closer through chastisement.

This is at first counter-intuitive. A tad distasteful. But the more we consider it, the sweeter it grows. And while there is much we could say biblically on this topic, let us first be quick to rejoice that God does not leave his children alone. He is thoroughly committed to the relationship, so much so that he is willing to bring hard things into our life that would drive us away from sin and unto him. Is it any wonder God is the perfect Father, loving his children so much that he will not let anything stand in the way of his divine parenting?

This should move us to think deeply about and look closely at our lives today. And while I'll be the first to contend that suffering is not always a sign something is wrong, I'll also be quick to remind us that suffering may very well be just that: a sign from God to come back to him. In light of God's Word, what is the Holy Spirit saying to you today through your situation?

In both the Old and New Testaments, there are examples of sickness, hardship, and difficulty being used, even ordained, by God for the purpose of turning the attention of his people from spiritual idolatry to spiritual monogamy (Deut. 28, I Cor. 11, 1 John 5). So we shouldn't be surprised when God actively interrupts our life with discipline. Why? Because God rightfully and jealously desires to know his people and be known by his people. And he will do everything to ensure that occurs.

Rejoice today, my brother or sister! In the good and the bad, your Heavenly Father is actively working to draw you closer so that "you will know that I am the LORD."

Tuesday
Isaiah 65:24

Wednesday
John 12:32

Thursday
Jeremiah 32:17

Friday
John 17:3

Saturday/Sunday
Jeremiah 9:23-24

"God was bringing his people closer through chastisement."

WEEK 43
The Common Question We Should Ask

Jesus' last words ought to prompt us towards a first question: Who are you discipling?

Imagine if this was the common question among our gathering, in our small groups, throughout our individual conversations, and around the dinner table? Just think of the missional drift we'd prevent, both personally and congregationally, if Christ's final words, which are in each of the first five books of the New Testament (Matthew 28:16-20, Mark 16:15, Luke 20; John 20:21, Acts 1:8), were our first concern in our everyday conversations. This simple question—Who are you discipling? —is a game changer when it permeates the conversational and relational culture of a church.

I wonder if one reason more of us don't ask this question proactively is because most of us don't want to be asked this question personally. Admittedly, it can seem initially uncomfortable to have a friend ask us for something so specific and straightforward—a name. An actual person we know and are spiritually developing so they will do the same in the future. Yet, that's precisely the intentionality needed in order for the disciplemaking to be normal, not novel.

To move the disciplemaking needle from novel to normal, consider this two-fold challenge today. Commit to 1) answering that question, then 2) asking that question. Start with yourself, then work outward with your closest relationships. Inquire of those with whom you are the safest first. They'll hear you well, and will engage in a fruitful conversation probably.

Then, begin humbly asking others with whom you are relationally connected this same question. And ask this question, not as a test, but as a prompt. Do so to elevate the topic of disciplemaking, making it normal to talk personally, not merely conceptually, about our one job as Christians and as a church.

Multiplication will always seem a million miles away until we move towards personalizing the mandate of the Great Commission with concrete names. Becoming a people ready to reproduce will only be collectively palpable when we get individually comfortable with this question being common: Who are you discipling?

Tuesday
2 Timothy 2:2

Wednesday
Luke 6:40

Thursday
1 Corinthians 11:1

Friday
Hebrews 10:24-25

Saturday/Sunday
Philippians 2:3-4

"Multiplication will always seem a million miles away until we move towards personalizing the mandate of the Great Commission with concrete names."

WEEK 44
Start Where You Are

The Jerusalem church of Acts 2, led by the very men who heard the final instructions of Jesus, were a missional band of believers. They did exactly what they were told to do: make disciples of all nations.

Luke not only records this endeavor in his historical account "The Acts of the Apostles," but he provides other insight in this same book that gives both a descriptive pattern and the prescriptive principles for mission and missions.

What we see, essentially, is a model of mission and missions that has three dimensions: a geographical dimension, a logistical dimension, and a spiritual dimension. Thus, one could say the first church operated in a "3D environment" regarding mission and missions.

Likewise, these three dimensions (geographical, logistical, and spiritual) provide for us a very biblical way to go about the mission of the church, and for sure the missions of the church. In short, these dimensions could be defined in three short sentences: Start where you are, use what you have, send who the Spirit selects.

Concerning the first dimension, I find it intriguing that often we assume those first disciples went somewhere else. But they didn't. They simply started where they already were—in Jerusalem. In fact, the word "go" in Matthew 28:19 is best rendered "as you are going." Combine this with Acts 1:8, where they are told they will be witnesses in Jerusalem, and the plain sense is that they were to be going about their life in a natural way but with a supernatural power, the kind of power that enabled them to be disciple-making witnesses right where they already were.

Admittedly, they were witnesses to all different kinds of people, but at least initially this did not happen in all kinds of different places. Rather, it started right where they were.

What we see is a rippling of their influence, predicted by Jesus in fact. And just as assuredly as Acts 1:8 lays out what they're to do, it also assured them of what God would do.

And Acts chronicles precisely this "rippling effect" of the early church. Acts 2-7 showcases the witness in Jerusalem, Acts 8-12 highlights the witness in Judea and Samaria, and Acts 13-28 details the witness to the end of the earth.

Today, start where you are. Be missional where you are already planted. Make disciples in your current context. That really is the essence of "going"—it's an action you are already undertaking. So make the most of your movement today by making disciples wherever you are already going.

Yes, start where you are.

Tuesday
Mark 16:15

Wednesday
Romans 10:14-15

Thursday
Matthew 5:16

Friday
Acts 5:42

Saturday/Sunday
Matthew 9:37-38

"The plain sense is that they were going about their life in a natural way but with a supernatural power, the kind of power that enabled them to be disciple-making witnesses right where they already were."

WEEK 45
Use What You Have

Mission is always, first and foremost, an issue of motivation, not means.

Case in point: the Jerusalem church of Acts. While the eleven disciples and the early church could have wished they had more resources to accomplish the job of making disciples of all nations, they didn't. Instead, they simply and obediently started where they were with who and what they had.

This is the essence of the logistical dimension of both the mission and missions: using who and what you have. Truly missional followers aren't waiting till the right person comes along, the best tool is found, or the golden opportunity present itself. They size up what they have available and seize the moment. They don't see logistics—or the lack of them—as a means of limiting their movement, but rather as a means of leveraging for momentum.

Frankly, the early church, still reeling from 50 days of amazingly life-altering and eyebrow-raising events (i.e., Christ's crucifixion, resurrection, and ascension), cleared some high hurdles in their first few weeks. From appointing Mathias to replace Judas to meeting in an upstairs room to utilizing homes for gathering to baptizing thousands in rivers to sharing resources and selling property to finding men to help with widows, the early church didn't wait till everything was "in place" to begin making disciples. The task was simply and supernaturally thrust upon them, and they responded by using who they had and what they had immediately. Willingly. Generously.

Clearly, all were in because all were needed. This is what the Great Commission requires—all of us "all in."

Today, stop delaying giving because you're waiting till you have more to give; give what you have. Quit procrastinating inviting your friend to church; send that text or make that call today with an invitation for this weekend. No longer delay in opening your home to your neighbors; swing those doors wide today and show hospitality to those closest to you. Refuse to put off taking time off to go on that mission trip; commit today to experiencing the foreign field.

In short, look at what you have, then use it for God's mission. Resist focusing on what you don't have; rather, utilize what you do have. Think participation and progress, nor perfection.

After all, there will never be a perfect time to be on-mission; there will only be the right time. And the right time is now.

Tuesday
1 Thessalonians 4:12

Wednesday
Philippians 2:12-16

Thursday
Romans 1:5

Friday
1 Corinthians 14:24-25

Saturday/Sunday
Acts 8:4-5

"This is what the Great Commission requires—all of us 'all in.'"

WEEK 46
Send Who the Spirit Selects

A church's best pool for partners (i.e., missionaries/church planters) is its own body, and the best practice for finding them is prayer.

This is one of the key takeaways from Acts 13, the account of Paul and Barnabas being sent by the church in Antioch. What is intriguing is the manner, or way, in which they were selected and sent: by the Holy Spirit through the church's leaders.

Specifically, it was during worship and prayer that the church recognized this divine "setting apart" and then responded by affirming and sending. While there is probably more that happened procedurally and logistically than we are told in the text, the emphasis is quite clear—it was people within their own faith family that were called by God's Spirit to go and make disciples of all nations somewhere else. And they did.

This was not, however, the first "sending" to occur in Acts. By Acts 8 persecution had scattered most of the initial church, an informal sending no doubt. And God the Holy Spirit did select specific people from their own midst to go to other places even before Paul and Barnabas departed Antioch (Acts 8, 10, and Acts 11). "Go into all the world and make disciples of all nations" was not simply an idealistic statement Jesus made; it was an actual and historical, even prophetic, promise concerning what would happen in the lives of his disciples in multiple ways.

What resulted from this specific effort of formal and informal "sending?" Communities of new disciples. Or, in plain terms, churches. In fact, much of the New Testament is the letters written to the churches planted by the first missionaries. Which is why we believe the end-game of missions (i.e., making disciples of all nations) is church planting. And where do church planters come from? Ideally, from among ourselves.

Today, joyfully embrace God's passion for his glory among the nations, and humbly submit to his commitment to selecting and sending specific ones from among us to go to other places to continue making disciples of all nations so that churches are planted. This is the heartbeat of a people who are ready to reproduce—a willingness to send whom the Holy Spirit selects.

Tuesday
John 16:13-14

Wednesday
Acts 1:8

Thursday
Ephesians 5:18

Friday
Acts 9:31

Saturday/Sunday
Romans 8:26

"It was during worship and prayer that the church recognized this divine 'setting apart' and then responded by affirming and sending."

WEEK 47
The Adrenaline god

When Scripture speaks of the pace at which we are to live as Christians, the word picture is overwhelmingly one of steadiness. Faithfulness. Consistency. It's not one of high-speed adrenaline or hurriedness.

For example, Paul urged gospel servants in Corinth "to be found faithful" (1 Cor. 4:2) and citizens in Thessalonica to "aspire to live quietly, and to mind your own affairs" (1 Thess. 4:11); the writer of Hebrews exhorted dispersed believers to "run with endurance the race that is set before us" (Hebrews 12:1); Paul reminded Timothy to "be ready in season and out of season" (2 Tim 4:2), the Romans to "be patient in affliction" (Romans 12:12), and the Christians in Galatia to "not grow weary in doing good" (Galatians 6:9). These are but a few of the imperatives that call us to a life of righteous routines.

Our current culture, however, pushes against these concepts. "Itching ears" too often sadly characterizes our disguised desire for the newest thrill or spiritual high. We too quickly grow bored with the tried-and-true and falsely think the flashy and shiny will finally satisfy our souls. We search for an in-the-moment rush or a once-in-a-lifetime adventure to produce a non-stop flow of adrenaline. "Maybe that will get me where I need to be," we think. The reality is this: It won't. It never has. And it never will.

Instead of chasing the dream at breakneck pace, let me encourage you to strengthen the stride of your daily steps. Walking surely is far better than running blindly. Accuracy is much more valuable than adrenaline. Plodding your way there is of greater worth than quickly projecting yourself there. "Slow and steady wins the race" is a well-worn phrase for a reason: It's true.

If you're wondering if you're chasing an adrenaline god or following the Almighty God, consider three diagnostic questions:

- Do you sense a lot of motion (i.e., external activity) but little progress (i.e., internal change)?
- Does your calendar dictate your schedule more than God's mission?
- Is your spiritual growth based on events and programs or disciplines and relationships?

As you ponder the previous questions, commit to focusing today on the steps God has before you in this moment. Surrender each one singly and specifically to the Lord as he "orders them" (Psalm 37:23). Yoke up with him as he leads you through the fields of your life, discipling you gently and slowly each step of the way in his manners and mindsets.

Remember, fellow sheep, following is better than chasing.

Tuesday
Micah 6:8

Wednesday
Galatians 5:16

Thursday
2 Corinthians 5:7

Friday
Psalm 119:133

Saturday/Sunday
Isaiah 30:21

"Walking surely is far better than running blindly."

WEEK 48
Our Confident Hope

"I sure hope so."

Those are the words that express our wants and wishes. And there's nothing wrong with them. Every human has temporal things they rightfully desire and for which they long. And while many of those very things are out of our control, we still hope. Even when the odds seem against us and the "chances" are low, we cling to hope, holding on to our wishes and wants.

But for the Christian, hope is far more than wishes and wants about temporal things. It is a confidence in God about eternal things. Namely, the coming of his kingdom and the righting of all wrongs. Our hope in that future reality rests, not on chances and coincidence, but on the unfailing promises of God.

In fact, the promise that he will come *again* is rooted in the fact that he already came *once*. The promise that his kingdom will be *consummated* is rooted in the fact that it has already been *initiated*.

For centuries the Old Testament writers predicted the coming of the Messiah, assuring Israel and other nations that they weren't waiting in futility, but rather in confident hope. Consider Isaiah 7:14: "Therefore the Lord himself will give you a sign: The virgin will conceive and give birth to a son, and will call him Immanuel." Just as promised, Christ came, the hope of the world and the fulfillment of all God promised. (Luke 1:35; Matthew 4:17; 2 Cor. 1:20)

So when Jesus himself and the New Testament writers comfort us with the promise of his second coming (John 14:3 and Hebrews 9:28 to name two), it isn't based on mere chance or circumstantial likelihood. Quite the contrary! It is founded on the character of God who has kept all of his promises throughout history in actual time and space and will most certainly keep them all the way to the end.

That's why the biblical hope is far stronger than cultural hope. It is far more than living with our spiritual fingers crossed. It is living with our hearts set most assuredly and confidently, not on what we can produce, but on what God has promised—his kingdom come! That's much greater than a "I sure hope so." That's a "Because he said so."

This week, as Advent begins, "set your hope fully on the grace to be given you when Jesus Christ is revealed" (1 Peter 1:13). Celebrate his first coming, and may it lead you to anticipate confidently his second coming.

Tuesday
Romans 12:12

Wednesday
Isaiah 40:31

Thursday
Romans 8:24-25

Friday
Psalm 39:7

Saturday/Sunday
Psalm 119:114

"Hope is living with our hearts set most assuredly and confidently, not on what we can produce, but on what God has promised—his kingdom come!"

BONUS MIDWEEK MEDITATION
A Common Christmas

Christmas has too quickly been hijacked by the commercial world and the postmodern consumer. It's "the most wonderful time of the year," but for all the wrong reasons. Instead of a virgin and a manger, we've been given a Santa and a sleigh ride. Consequently, the journey back to the first nativity can get fuzzy. Inappropriately simple. Too easy.

Hear me out – I'm not arguing for undermining Christmas as we know it. Seriously, I love the Christmas traditions our family has enjoyed over the years, such as a zillion lights on the house, Christmas music playing 24/7 the day after Thanksgiving, traveling to MI or TN, and Julie's famous and delicious lasagna on Christmas night. Count me in on all of that!

What I'm urging us to do is understand Christmas as they knew it. For that initial Christmas no doubt looked really different. No river and woods on the way to grandmother's house; probably more like a hilly dirt road heading south out of Jerusalem. No angel named Clarence; more like an angel named Gabriel. And no coming home parties from the hospital; instead, a quick escape to a totally different country.

Yet, in many ways, it probably looked very similar. I'm sure they were afraid of the unknown, just like we are. I suspect they were nervous about facing tough circumstances, just like we are. I bet they had to find a way to look ahead even when their past seemed to pull them back, just like we do. In many ways, Christmas has common themes, such as hope, peace, joy, and love.

Thus, the Advent journey. That's the journey I invite you to take during December; those are the common steps in which I hope you'll walk again this year as you relive the hope that God provided for Mary (Luke 1:26-38), the peace the Lord brought to Joseph (Matt. 1:20-25), the joy that overcame Zechariah (Luke 1:67-79), and the love that was shown to the world (John 3:16).

Resist the holiday pull of society and remember the Christmas pictures of Scripture as you reflect and rejoice in anticipation of Christ's coming. Those are the timeless and treasured snapshots, rooted in history, that will help each of us every Christmas. Truly, as we understand their journey, I think we'll be able to better undertake ours.

"Resist the holiday pull of society and remember the Christmas pictures of Scripture, reflecting and rejoicing in anticipation of Christ's coming."

WEEK 49
Our Indescribable Peace

Peace. An internal calm in the middle of an external storm.

Even that definition sounds unexplainable, almost contradictory. But such is the wonderful nature of peace. At least true, biblical peace.

No wonder Paul would describe biblical peace with the words "which surpasses all understanding" (Phil. 4:7). God supernaturally enables his children to experience divine calm when there is distracting, even dysfunctional, chaos all around us. In those moments, we find it humanly impossible to verbalize how two completely different situations can exist simultaneously. Yet, they can when the peace of God is present.

Remember when Jesus walked on the water towards the disciples who were struggling to keep their boat from capsizing in the storm? They were unquestionably frightened. But when Jesus entered the boat, He commanded the wind and the waves to be still, bringing peace to both the elements of weather and his students. His presence brought unexplainable peace, an indescribable calm in an undesirable storm.

Additionally, peace is exactly what the angels announced to the shepherds on the night of Christ's birth. Yet, it wasn't a peaceful time in that region, including Bethlehem. Instead, it was a time of registration and taxation required by a foreign occupying force. Specifically for Mary and Joseph, the long travel and crowded conditions, mixed with pregnancy, undoubtedly created much stress for them. It was in the middle of all of this that angel knew exactly what was needed: peace brought by the presence of the Christ child.

The point is quite clear—without the presence of Jesus, there is no unexplainable peace. Oh, there may be temporary agreement, even a level of "getting along" that suffices for the short term. But it's not peace that lasts or the kind of soul rest that exists in the middle of external distress. That kind of peace can only come from God.

And it did when Jesus came. And it will when Jesus comes again. This isn't saying we don't experience this peace powerfully now through the Holy Spirit. Yes, we do. But when he comes again, we will experience it personally, just as they did when he came the first time.

During this advent season, may you internally know the indescribable peace of God in the middle of externally undesirable circumstances. For Jesus has come with "peace among those with whom he is pleased" (Luke 2:14).

Tuesday
Isaiah 26:3

Wednesday
2 Thessalonians 3:16

Thursday
John 14:27

Friday
Psalm 29:11

Saturday/Sunday
Isaiah 9:6

"God supernaturally enables his children to experience divine calm when there is distracting, even dysfunctional, chaos."

BONUS MIDWEEK MEDITATION
Have Yourself a Messy Little Christmas

Christmas is a messy holiday. I didn't say merry; I said messy. Think about it—it's about a birth. Been to any birthing rooms lately? Well, Joseph's and Mary's was outdoors in a holed-out animal shelter. See what I mean? Messy!

But no wonder—Parenting is messy. So it's fitting it starts that way on day one. Remember your first child's birth! Whew, it was a rude awakening for yours truly!

And the messiness of children continues. And I don't just mean logistically or physically. But emotionally. Psychologically. Spiritually. There's no way around it—children are messy!

Yet, no real parent would trade the messiness of children for the cleanliness of loneliness. Why? Because it's in the mess that we're blessed! That's right—the blessedness is in the messiness. For it's when we get our hands dirty that we do more than eye a work of God. We experience it.

Recall the manger in the holed-out animal shelter? God coming to earth via the birth canal amid an audience of animals. No doubt that was a hands-on experience for Joseph and Mary. No doubt a blessed mess!

No other verse describes the blessedness of messiness better than John 1:14: "The Word became flesh and made his dwelling among us." Now that's a messy verse! Literally, the language could read he "pitched his tent" among us. Not just near us. Not just by us. But among us. Right smack dab in the middle of us.

Yeah, us—the liars, stealers, backbiters, lusters, enviers, haters, murderers, adulterers, rebellious, proud, complainers, lazy, and addicted—us! That's where he landed. Pretty messy, huh? That's Jesus!

But the arrival of the Blessed One among us messy ones is grand news! Why? He's the only one who can do what needs to be done about the mess we're in—save us from it! To be more precise, the sin that has separated us from God has been defeated by the One who came as a baby. His sacrificial and substitutionary death has satisfied the wrath of God against sin, and all who believe are no longer buried in condemnation, but blessed by justification. No wonder the news to the shepherds that night, even in the middle of herding messy sheep, and sung by a host of angels in the midnight sky, was "glory to God in the highest, and on earth peace among those with whom he is pleased" (Luke 2:14). God had come to earth, in the middle of a mess no doubt, to actually do something about it—bless us!

So get your hands dirty this Christmas. Involve yourself in a mess for the sake of Christ and his gospel. Pitch your tent among those who have yet to see the real meaning of Christmas. Live incarnationally and intentionally in the middle of a situation that desperately needs the grace of God seen and heard through a gospel-centered voice and life. Jesus did on the first one. And we've all been blessed ever since.

> **"God had come to earth, in the middle of a mess no doubt, to actually do something about it—bless us."**

WEEK 50
Our Unspeakable Joy

Joy. It's the emotion that goes public. When you experience it, other people usually know it.

Sometimes we shout because of our joy, like at a game or athletic event. Other times we share because of our joy, like at the birth of a child—"It's a girl!" Or when we got engaged. Still at other times we sing because of our joy, belting out a melody from the bottom of our heart. In so many ways, joy inevitably bursts forth—is expressed—in words when the heart is full.

Yet, the Bible describes a type of joy that is inexpressible.

Wait a minute—a joy that is impossible to put into words? Yes! Odd as it may seem, that's the thought behind 1 Peter 1:8 where Peter states that God's people, when they think about the Lord whom they haven't seen but believe and love and can't wait to see, "rejoice with joy that is inexpressible and filled with glory."

Those ten words are life altering! To think that we could have such an incredibly deep and high response of joy that we aren't able to articulate it in words makes my head spin. Or that we could long for Jesus' return with such weighty and passionate anticipation that we aren't able to express it in the language we know—hard to imagine being that speechless.

But such is the result of truly embracing Advent. As we meditate upon our Lord's first coming, then wait eagerly for his second coming, I am convinced we will find ourselves at a loss for words. It's inspired silence, not due to nothing to say, but because there is so much to say. So much that we don't know where to start.

It's the kind of response that isn't only breathtaking, but, according to Peter, "word taking" as well.

Keep in mind this kind of response doesn't indicate a loss of joy, but quite the opposite—a fullness of joy. A joy that is all-consuming, so much so that verbal descriptions and exclamations escape us. They, too, are consumed in the moment of rapturous delight where our tongues get tied and our souls get stirred by the One we have come to trust and desire to see; the One in whom we have placed all our faith regarding what is and what is to come. That's joy inexpressible.

Please don't think Peter is saying we shouldn't express our joy. Sure we should! Whenever you can, shout, share, and sing to the glory of the Lord. Let your heart exult in Christ your Savior verbally. Visually. Loudly. Without apology.

But when you experience moments when the joy is so pervasive that it overrides even normal pronunciation, take heart—it's still joy. Undeniable joy. Simply inexpressible joy. May that kind of joy rise up in us regularly, leaving us in awe and wonder of the Christ who has come and will come again.

Tuesday
Philippians 4:4

Wednesday
Psalm 16:11

Thursday
John 15:11

Friday
John 16:22

Saturday/Sunday
Jeremiah 15:16

"Joy is the kind of response that isn't only breathtaking, but, according to Peter, 'word taking' as well."

BONUS MIDWEEK MEDITATION
The Hidden Beauty of Significance

The beauty of significance lies in the fact that it is often hidden in the ugliness of the seemingly unimportant.

This was exactly the case on that first Christmas centuries ago. Who would have thought a little town would be the birthplace of a mighty king? Or that this mighty king would choose a lowly stable as his birthplace? Or that simple shepherds would be the first avenue for blasting the news? So much about Christmas is counter-intuitive. Ironic. Paradoxical. Odd. Initially seemingly unimportant. But actually, in the end, it was all eternally significant. Beautiful. Meaningful.

I suspect gifts are often that way as well. What we sometimes think is unimportant actually proves to be essential. I know this from experience, for as a Jr. Higher, when I really wanted the new handheld electronic football game for Christmas, what I got instead was an electric blanket. Seriously? That's what I thought as a puberty-riddled middle schooler. Talk about disappointment.

I still remember it. Our entire family and extended family always congregated at my grandparents home in Tucker, GA, and hours of getting reacquainted, as well as grazing on Christmas goodies and gift-opening, was the reason. That year was no exception. You know, that year when the fad and craze for 14 year-olds was the multi-button, 6-light, handheld electric football game? Yeah, that year. When my turn rolled around, I was so sure I would open that big box and find that it was only extreme packaging to disguise the real treasure inside—that multi-button, 6-light, handheld electronic football game (which was an upgrade from the 4-light version the year before). I ripped that box open, eager as could be, only to discover that the box was actually not a disguise at all. Inside was something electric alright—an electric blanket. My first thought? I opened the wrong box. But no, that was my gift, in all of its weird wonder and mystery.

Yet, decades later, when that football game was a long-forgotten dinosaur, guess what was keeping my kids warm on a cold Iowa night? You got it—that seemingly unimportant electric blanket. In hindsight, that may have been one of the more beautiful gifts I've ever received.

Such is the case for things like humility, security, simplicity. They seem unattractive at first. Almost unnecessary. Unimportant. Yet, those are actually the significant gifts that prove so vital eventually. Crucial. Yes, beautiful.

This Christmas, set your heart to discover the hidden beauty of seemingly insignificant gifts, like the baby of a teenage virgin who came to us in an almost unnoticeable fashion 2000 years ago in Bethlehem. For it's the small things that make the largest difference, especially when his name is Jesus.

"What we sometimes think is unimportant actually proves to be essential."

WEEK 51
God's Unconditional Love

God's love is qualitatively and quantitatively different than our love. Need proof? Consider the first part of 1 John 3:1.

> "See what kind of love the Father has given to us, that we should be called children of God; and so we are."

When John wrote "what kind of love," he was literally referring to it as "other worldly love," indicating it's not something we've humanly known or seen. And for good reason—because of God's love, we have been brought into the family of God. What an incredible and miraculous reality that spiritual enemies of God can actually become spiritual "children of God." No wonder his response to this kind of love was "See!" One translation begins this verse with the word, "Behold." In our common vernacular, we'd probably say, "Stop and take a look at this!" No matter how you slice it, John is calling for a long look at the love of God.

Why? Because no other love goes to such dramatically great lengths for those are the epitome of unlovely. Think about it—God moved towards us when we we're fighting against him. God reached out to us when we were rejecting him. God wanted the best for us when we were at our worst. God did everything necessary to save those who were doing everything to sin. That's the kind of love he has for us: unconditional.

It's this unconditional love that is at the root of God's redemptive actions. John says this is why he sent his only Son (John 3:16), and Paul asserted this is why Christ died for us (Romans 5:8) and why God made us alive with Christ (Ephesians 2:5). These cornerstone actions of salvation were not aimed at people who were deserving or worthy, individuals who had earned some type of divine extra credit. They were on behalf of the weak, the ungodly, and the sinful (Romans 5:6-8). There were no conditions that needed met before God would love us. He loved us out of his own compassion, what the Bible calls his "rich mercy" and "great love" (Ephesians 2:4).

When we look long at this kind of love from God, we will begin to be motivated by it. It will begin to "control us" (2 Cor. 5:14), enabling us to love more and more like God—unconditionally. To love, not just in word, but "in deed and in truth" (1 John 3:18). We will notice a proactive spirit welling up within us to take loving action in spite of who people are, not just because of who people are.

As Advent draws to a close this week, savor the unconditional love of God that was showcased in the first coming of Jesus, God's only Son. Let it sink deeply down into your soul, recalibrating how you love and live while you wait with eagerness for his second coming.

Tuesday
1 John 4:18

Wednesday
John 3:16

Thursday
Romans 5:8

Friday
1 John 3:16

Saturday/Sunday
Isaiah 49:15-16

"There were no conditions that needed met before God would love us. He loved us out of his own compassion."

BONUS MIDWEEK MEDITATION
God With Us

Today we rejoice in the fulfillment of our anticipation. Advent is realized; Jesus has come. Yes, Immanuel is here.

Ah, Immanuel. It means "God with us." Those three incredible words teach us much about our Lord's "with-us-ness." And my mind and heart have been massaged by the truth contained in them. Follow along for a minute.

"God" expresses the truth of deity. Yes, at Christmas, God came near. It wasn't merely a prophet or just a good man that descended to earth. It was God. And it wasn't a son of God, but the Son of God. That's who Jesus is – God! What a truth to celebrate: That at Christmas, Deity came to earth!

"Us" expresses the truth of humanity. At Christmas, Jesus became one of us! Not just someone close to us, or someone kind of like us. No, he became one of us in every way, even someone lower on the cultural chain than what most of us would want to be— He became a servant! In one doctrinal word, it's the incarnation. God becoming flesh. And it's at the heart of Christmas!

Philippians 2:6-7 gives us a further glimpse into God's "withusness" when it says, "[Jesus], being in very nature God, did not consider equality with God something to be grasped, but made himself nothing, taking the very nature of a servant, being made in human likeness..."

Here's the best part: Combine deity and humanity and something supernatural is accomplished for every single person who repents and believes in the God-man: Eternity with him!

Make no mistake: Eternal life is the gracious gift because Deity and humanity came together! Yes, "God with us" means that for all who believe, it is "us with God" forever! Truly, once we believe the truth about Immanuel, these words hold great promise no matter the order. What a reason to celebrate "God with us" – that "us with God" is now the reality for all who trust in Christ!

"'God with us' means that for all who believe, it is 'us with God' forever!"

WEEK 52
Clamped, Ramped, and Cramped

Christmas is now in your rear-view mirror.

Often, post-holiday emotions set in about now and we find ourselves, whether personally, relationally, financially, or occupationally, living clamped, ramped and cramped just after singing the last chorus of "Joy to the World." Let me explain.

By the end of December, we're usually running on less time, less money, and less energy. This squeeze usually means we feel a tightening effect on our calendars, wallets, and stamina. So we clamp up (or down) a bit. Maybe a lot.

Add to that the fact that a new year is staring us in the face, and things start ramping up, too! People and groups are trying to nail down all kinds of things, from next year's schedules to next year's deductions to next year's plans. Seems as though everybody wants a decision yesterday about tomorrow.

Here's the rub. Those details can cramp our various relationships. And since we don't normally deal with that many details in such a compressed amount of time, we aren't especially experienced at handling it. We respond too quickly, speak too harshly, ask too insultingly, or decide too rashly. What suffers? Not the details. Instead, the relationships.

Not to beat this drum too much, but I've seen this happen in my life and work more than I want to admit. For instance, my wife and I will be working through an end-of -year issue when, suddenly, a simple difference of opinion about a small thing shuts down the whole conversation. Or I'm hammering out financial forecasts for the upcoming year with one of our leadership teams and, almost without warning, tensions thicken and people start being silent.

At the root of this relational post-holiday hemorrhaging, at least in my opinion, is the selfish need to control and manipulate the final elements of the current year. Sure, this is a constant problem in humans, but I think we all want to "finish on top," so for some reason division can be especially tempting at year's end. It's like we think the party ends December 31 and we have to have the silver slipper when the clock strikes midnight.

A simple tip has helped me over and over: Look to contribute, not control. Ask questions that center on how you can help, not on why you think every detail is being hindered. Frankly, if one has to have his or her way in every decision or situation in which they are involved, it shouldn't be surprising when people start pulling away relationally. If one has to always share his or her opinion and "be heard," they'll probably find themselves with no one to talk to at some point. If, as the year draws to a close, one has to make a "last stand" every time they turn around, they'll probably end up feeling like Custer at Little Big Horn.

I'm not suggesting we become spineless, never expressing strong opinions. But let's agree that at this time of year, it's especially crucial to do it in a way—and at a time—when it isn't relational suicide. Let's put Colossians 3:12-13 into practice more than ever, which exhorts us, as God's chosen ones, to "put on compassion, kindness, humility, gentleness, and patience, bearing with one another and forgiving one another if anyone has a grievance against another."

Bottom line? The week following Christmas is the best time to go into your conversations and encounters knowing that, for whatever reason, people may be just a little more "clamped" and "ramped." So *bear with one another*—speak and act in ways that relieve relational "cramps." Think twice before you correct a technicality. Count to a million before you demand uniformity. Wait one more minute before developing an assumption. In light of all the end-of-year details merging together in one seven day period, you—and others around you—will be glad you did.

Tuesday
Ephesians 4:29

Wednesday
James 1:19-20

Thursday
Galatians 5:22-23

Friday
Proverbs 14:29

Saturday/Sunday
1 Corinthians 13:4-5

"At this time of year, it's especially crucial to share opinions in a way—and at a time—when it isn't relational suicide."

WEEK 53
All Comfort > Any Affliction

There's no hardship greater than the comforting hand of God.

This biblical promise is based on four words I find in 2 Corinthians 1: "all comfort" (v 3) and "any affliction" (v 4).

Take a minute and read it for yourself.

"Blessed be the God and Father of our Lord Jesus Christ, the Father of mercies and God of all comfort, who comforts us in all our affliction, so that we may be able to comfort those who are in any affliction, with the comfort with which we ourselves are comforted by God."

Essentially, Paul assured those Corinthian believers that God's comfort, which comes to and through people, would always be enough for any of their hardships. Always.

That truth is still valid today. God's comfort, which comes to and through people, is always enough for any of our hardships. Always.

Know what that means? It means that

- Sad surprises which suddenly change your life don't dismiss God's comfort.
- Death's temporary separation doesn't end God's comfort.
- A sudden sickness won't weaken God's comfort.
- A terminal illness can't stop God's comfort.
- Cultural opposition doesn't intimidate God's comfort.
- Relational tension won't silence God's comfort.
- Emotional trauma can't scare God's comfort.
- A sketchy past can't erase God's comfort.

- An uncertain future won't conceal God's comfort.

In other words, all of God's comfort is greater than any of your affliction. In mathematical terms, "all God's comfort" > "any of your affliction." And note the modifiers, would you? They are especially captivating because they are not accidental. Rather, they are quite intentional.

Why? Perhaps it's because Paul was aware his readers were people of "exceptions." Much like you and me, they may have thought, "God's comfort is good for them but not for me." Or, "it helps for that, but not for this." Yet, two simple words—"all" and "any"—remove every exception and prove there is no hardship outside of or greater than the comforting hand of God. Not a single one.

So whatever you're facing today—that's right, whatever!—it isn't bigger, larger, greater, deeper, wider, stronger, or more powerful than the comfort that comes from God. You can be sure our Father's divine encouragement will always be more than enough for anything and everything that lies ahead of you.

"Therefore, we are comforted." (2 Cor. 7:13)

Tuesday
Matthew 11:28-30

Wednesday
Psalm 119:76

Thursday
Isaiah 49:13

Friday
Psalm 73:26

Saturday/Sunday
Revelation 21:4

"Two simple words—'all' and 'any'—remove every exception and prove there is no hardship outside of or greater than the comforting hand of God."

About the Author

Todd Stiles (PhD, Carolina University) is Lead Pastor at First Family Church in Ankeny, Iowa. He also serves as a church-based Church Planting Catalyst for the North American Mission Board (NAMB), helps in various roles with the Baptist Convention of Iowa (BCI), is on the board of The Daniel Project, and is currently a member of the SBC's Executive Committee. He writes at www.ToddStiles.net, and is the author of several other books, including *Home Run: Family, Baseball, and Psalm 128;* and *Different, Not Just Better: Salvation in Street Clothes.*

Made in USA - North Chelmsford, MA
41990_9798860651654
12.09.2023 0518